The Complete
Driver

The Complete Driver

Clarence Beedle

To order additional copies of this book, contact:
Xlibris Corporation
1-888-7-XLIBRIS
www.Xlibris.com
Orders@Xlibris.com

Contents

TO ALL THE ADVANCED DRIVING INSTRUCTORS AND STUDENTS WHOM I HAVE HAD THE SINCERE PLEASURE OF WORKING WITH. ALTHOUGH I SUSPECT YOU DIDN'T ALWAYS SEE IT THAT WAY. WHAT I HAVE LEARNED FROM YOU OVER THE YEARS IS ON THE PAGES OF THIS BOOK. DRIVE SAFE!

Chapter One

THE WHY QUIZ

Actually, this is the introduction but because no one reads the introduction, I put it here, because you need to read it.

This book breaks all the rules. I am not a writer by profession. I am an advanced driver-training instructor by profession. I know I am supposed to introduce myself and put you in awe of my background, but that type of introduction has never appealed to me. If I can not attract your attention by what I have to say and how I say it, then I shouldn't be here talking to you. For me, the only credible measure of any instructor, is the subsequent response and performance of those receiving the instruction.

If the time we spend together on the pages of this book does not improve your driving skill, we were entertaining each other. That's not all bad but as an entertainer, I don't think I can hold your attention.

As an advanced driver training instructor, I think we're in for a good time.

I am not writing a book. I am talking to you and that is how I wish the book to proceed. It is not a 'how to book', it is a 'how you can book'. As such, I want it to be as interactive as we can possibly make it. I want you to ask questions aloud, and answer my questions aloud, as if we were together in person. Be a bit careful with that around strangers, lest they think you're nuts and call the police or want to know what it is you're smoking and where they can get some.

Please have pencil and paper readily available while reading because I am going to be asking you to answer questions and draw quick sketches.

"Wow"—Already we're not communicating. You are still reading and you don't have pencil or paper. Don't say that aloud! Just put the book down and go get paper and pencil. Thank you.

This is not a book you will read and put away. It is a training seminar on how you can improve your driving skills and thusly your chances of avoiding or surviving that suddenly unexpected driving emergency! This is a book you will refer to many times and pass on to a friend, because this discussion begins where other driving discussions normally end.

This is not a book about all you dumb drivers and how I am going to make you smarter. I don't know whom all those dumb drivers are that every one refers to—unless they are talking about us—and that couldn't be—because they are we.

I am not a doom and gloom instructor. I am an instructor who understands all the problems drivers face, because that has been my single point of focus for more years than I wish to think about.

Driving skill is not about steering in the direction of the skid. Driving skill is about understanding and anticipating everything there is to know about a skid, and correcting it while it happens! Teaching a person to correct a skid by a simple driving maneuver is like trying to teach a batter to hit a curve ball when it is already in the catcher's mitt!

A child can drive a car. That is, until something other than putting the car into motion and making it change direction should occur. However, isn't that also the case with licensed drivers, at certain unfortunate moments, which we refer to as accidents?

The physical skills required to operate a motor vehicle are relatively minimal in comparison to the mental skills needed. This is not some new kind of psychic philosophy. You don't have to shave your head or tattoo your body in order to follow the concept.

This concept is a compilation of years of experience, developing and implementing, advanced drivers training and then observing the students responses as an analysis of the effectiveness of the training.

If we have not taken the time to understand the concepts of a vehicle in motion how will we find the time during the driving emergency?

Please don't expect a lot of impressive statistics, mathematical equations, or engineering data. During those fractions of a second of the driving emergency, that information is totally meaningless to the driver trying to control the vehicle!

Don't expect "If this happens–You should do this" What you must do is–*Continue to drive your vehicle— until it is safe to do something other than that!*

To accomplish that, you must understand both the driver and the automobile and why they do, what they do, when they do it. Your driving skills will vastly improve and your chances of surviving that sudden, unexpected emergency will be greatly enhanced.

As we work our way through the different aspects of advanced driver training, we will be using the building block approach, where one section leads to and builds on another. If at times you are not quite sure where we're going, stick with me, and when we turn the corner you will know where you are.

You will not find any pictures, charts or graphs in this book. I am committed to the discussion format so you will have to draw your own pictures. By doing so you will demonstrate to yourself that *you* know your subject matter. Please keep the pencil and paper handy.

I will not try to impress you with my writing prose. In fact, my grammar and spelling checker program gave me a dismal rating. Then again, what does my computer know about driving! I know something about driving. This is my sandbox and it's about to become yours!

I would much prefer to address you in person, in a classroom seminar, but that would take more years than I have. We will have to do it on these pages and on your note pads. I hope you enjoy the experience, because I know I will as I always have.

Chapter One

THE "WHY" QUIZ

Why don't you have pencil and paper? (You didn't think I would notice?) (It would be good to write down your answers and set them aside for future comparison.)

Why do so many accidents occur at stop signs and intersections? (Ignore the obvious, it takes two or more to have a multi-car crash.)

Why are there so many serious and fatal crashes associated with a vehicle going off the side of the road? (I promised no statistics, but this is a serious problem, and sadly enough the majority of the time the seriousness could have been greatly reduced.)

Why do we continue to have so many major rear-end collisions? (Again, ignore the obvious and think about why the vehicle doing the colliding didn't turn away)

Why are skid control and hydroplaning, so often discussed and so much publicized?

Why do skids and hydroplaning result in so many serious crashes?

Why is correct tire inflation pressure important?

Why do under-inflated tires contribute to highway crashes?

Why does ABS, (Anti-Skid Braking System) work more effectively during emergency braking than a conventional braking system? (Does it?—under all conditions?)

Why was ABS engineered and installed on the automobile?

Why do so many, otherwise good drivers, suddenly "freeze-up" at the moment of the driving emergency?

Why is driver body position and hand placement on the steering wheel important to car control? (Think about this one, there is a lot of misunderstanding about this topic.)

For answers to the why quiz: *Read the book! There is a lot more to come and I promise to present it, in a manner easily understood and then applied.*

Chapter Two

"YOU AND THE AUTOMOBILE"

In this chapter, we are going to be discussing driver attitude. As soon as I said that, all of you have skipped to chapter three and I'm talking to myself. I didn't say I was going to lecture you about attitude, or tell you what yours should be.

What we are going to do is develop an understanding of WHY, attitude is important to driving skill. Then you can decide what yours should be. Thinking and believing something is so doesn't necessarily make it that way. Thinking and believing something is NOT so, will guarantee, for you, that it never will be that way. Denial may be a useful tool for some aspects of our lives. Denial is a dangerous and self-destructive tool, in life threatening situations.

Now please come back from chapter three. There is important information here and I think you will enjoy it, and I know you can benefit from it.

When I first began thinking about writing a book on advanced driving training, I mentioned it to a colleague. His instant response was; "You can't learn to drive by reading a book!"

My answer to that was "But every licensed driver already knows how to drive".

"Do they really now" was his final word. What do you think? Why don't we take a closer look, then decide. Under normal highway conditions, the act of driving an automobile is perceived by the average driver as relatively easy, almost boring, and sometimes frustrating.

However, when *the normal,* suddenly becomes, *The driving emergency*—the average driver, doesn't do well.

Did we suddenly forget how to drive? Alternatively, perhaps we didn't completely learn to begin with?

The vast majority of the driving public, in the United States, were taught how to put the car into motion, make it change direction and make it come to a stop under control. They were taught to do these things in accordance with safe driving techniques, defensive driving techniques, traffic control devices and traffic laws. We were informed about the risks and hazards and supplied with factual statistics to back up the warnings.

Then we were tested on what we had been taught and if we passed the test, we were drivers. We were just not complete drivers. Experience was supposed to complete the process. If this is true, and unfortunately it is; how and when is a driver supposed to gain experience about the driving emergency?

During the driving emergency is a dangerous and deadly time to gain experience. Those terrifying moments of the unexpected loss of control of your automobile are not at all conducive to learning.

Right now, I would hope that all of you are asking aloud. "So how are we supposed to learn?"

Will it do any good for me to point out that you already have been taught the most advanced defensive driving techniques available!

"OH Great!" "So what am I supposed to do when some drunk comes down the road the wrong way headed right at me?"

Not all crashes are caused by the drunk drivers. Over half the fatalities are caused by some other driving error.

"Boy that's reassuring!" "Now what if one of those dumb drivers you say aren't dumb, pulls out in front of me on the highway?"

Let's change the direction of this conversation. There is no point, in going deeper and deeper into all the things we all already know. I would like to ask you, how many drivers practice routinely or even remember, all the defensive driving techniques they were taught?

I know the answer to that question. It is not opinion. It is a highway fatality statistical fact. That's what brings us here so let's talk about those driving skills we can become proficient with, without having a bad wreck in order to gain experience.

Before we start discussing the dynamics of the automobile, we need to talk about the dynamics of the driver. How and what we think, seriously effects, how and what we do. This is especially true during those moments of extreme excitement or fear. So let's begin by looking at those moments, of fearful excitation, which lead to panic.

Imagine this. You are in a comfortable environment, focused on whatever you are doing, perhaps reading a book, watching TV, listening to music. Then a practical joker sneaks up behind you and pops a big balloon—BANG!!!

I think we all know how that feels and what happens to our bodies, as we are startled! Muscles are instantly tensed. To a point, we couldn't move at that moment if we wanted to. Vision is narrowed or blurred and our hearing is suppressed. As instantly as it occurred, it is over. Our muscles relax and everything is calm except maybe our nerves and our vocal cords as we address the perpetrator.

In layman's terms, here's how it works. If any of the senses tell the brain that a muscle action is required, such as, blink, run, jump, duck, the brain triggers body chemicals to cause the muscles to respond.

When the "BANG" occurred, without any warning or cognizance, one of our primary senses was drastically startled, which caused the brain to instantly trigger the chemical release, without any cognitive direction as to what the muscles were supposed to do! So they simply tightened up until the brain triggered the chemicals to relax them, or caused them to be used.

This is not theory. It may be an overly simplistic explanation, but it is what happens, to a greater or lesser degree, depending on the individual and the amount of startle. We are all familiar with the expressions, "Freeze up", "shocked", "speechless".

Let's pretend for a moment. Imagine it happening right now! Go ahead and tense up, squint your eyes, scrunch your head into your shoulders! Now let's imagine us behind the wheel of an automobile and let's experience the same thing.—Only this sudden startle doesn't just go bang and go away. It keeps on coming. It's a bad crash about to happen to you! At this frozen moment in time you are one hundred percent focused on the impending crash and your body is reacting as it did to the, BANG! Who is driving your automobile? At that precise moment, no one is!

Studies have been conducted and documented that indicated more than one third of the drivers faced with impending crash, made no attempt what so ever, to avoid. Do you now understand who was driving their cars, and why!

In the following chapters, we will talk about how to prevent ourselves, from becoming that type of a statistic.

For right now, let's go back to the "BANG" startle.

This time however, out of the corner of our eye, we detect the prankster about to "POP" the balloon.

The sound didn't change, nor was it diminished; yet, the effect was seriously negated because we saw it coming and knew what was about to happen. We were prepared mentally. The body chemicals began being released at that instant! Now they are working for us—instead of against us and we are already responding to the impending BANG by grabbing the balloon, or putting our hands over our ears. Whatever our response, we are doing something!

There has been sufficient research done on the startle thing, and it's effect on the body, that it is widely taught as a necessary defensive measure in countering impending hostility and violence.

An automobile crash about to happen, is a violent, hostile thing!

If you understand and believe what we just discussed then you have gained an invaluable part of a driving emergency experience.

In order to advance our physical skill capability, we have to understand that if we get "startled" by any driving situation, none of us will do very well. If we see it coming, even in the last fraction of a second we have a chance. If we expect it, know when and where to most expect it, look for it and see it in advance, the driving emergency can be reduced, to the act of driving.

The startle effect is real. So real, I chose to make it the first topic of discussion. All the driving skills we could ever develop can be instantly negated if we don't avoid the startle and the subsequent "Freeze up"! Don't kid yourself, it can happen to you and it can happen to me, IF WE LET IT!

While we are on the topic of mental attitude and preparedness, let's talk about how you think about your automobile, and WHY that is important to driving skill.

A great cook not only knows how to follow the recipe but also understands the ingredients. If you don't understand the ingredients, you can still cook, but your chances of doing well at the difficult recipes, the very first time, are extremely slim.

Out there on the highway, behind the wheel of your automobile, you may not get a second chance. Others may not either.

So let's understand the ingredients of the driver and the vehicle we are driving and that will make the recipe to the driving emergency much easier to follow, instinctively. The notion that multiple driving skills are required to do something as simple as applying the brakes correctly during a driving emergency is an idea that is difficult to accept for most drivers. You will see during the discussions that follow how this is true and how critical each skill is to car control skill as a whole. The complete driver will understand this, accept it and apply it.

No one can teach you the dynamics of the vehicle, and get you to understand them. Except you. They can be presented, and will be on pages to come, but you have to understand their importance and WHY, to master them. The same is true for all aspects of driving.

If your attitude towards the vehicle is casual or careless, so your driving will become. If you are absolutely enamoured with your car, everything on the road is going to be a threat and a distraction and you will become a prime candidate for committing road rage. If you are confused and uncertain about the automobile, your driving decisions and actions during the emergency will be the same. If you think all the defensive driving techniques you, sort of, learned, are for old people, guess what your driving habits will reflect?

Chapter Three

UNDERSTANDING WHAT MAKES IT GO.

I am not going to tell you that if you have a tire blow out, while driving down the highway, you should do this or do that. I am going to lead you through an in depth understanding of exactly what just happened, and then you can decide what must be done under all variety of different conditions. We will use the same method of discussion for all topics covered.

Please understand. I can't tell you exactly what you should do during any given driving emergency, and guarantee one hundred percent, it will be the correct thing to do, at that moment in time!

I could write an entire book on all the different scenarios I could create for having a blow out and what to do. Which tire? What type of vehicle? Front wheel drive or rear wheel drive? On a hill, or in a corner? On dry pavement, or wet, and on and on?

Then even if I wrote it all down, it wouldn't do you a bit of good during the driving emergency because there would not be time to go through it all to come up with the correct answer.

This I can tell you! Continue to drive the vehicle until it is safe, to do something else! How you accomplish that, will depend to the greatest extent, on what you know and understand about the vehicle.

During the driving emergencies that have occurred, there are no systems I know of to accurately determine how often, or when, the driver stopped driving and became a passenger. Were I to venture an estimate, it would be a very high percentage of the times a crash happened.

For right now, I am going to get off the soapbox and we will get down to some serious technical discussion, but let's have some fun doing it. I have never really embraced the notion that learning and discovery needed to be painful.

I have a question I want you to answer, so grab the pencil and paper.

Q. What ultimately, causes the vehicle to do, what we direct it to do?

Don't read on ahead!

Think about it!

Get your pencil and paper.

Write down all the answers you can possibly think of!

Don't write in the book!

**Play this game with me, and begin to under-
stand communication.**

**A basic premise of communicating: You can
not receive, when you are transmitting!**

**Make sure you have your answers before you
read on!**

I have asked this question more times than I can remember, while standing in front of a group of advanced driving students. It has never ceased to amaze
me how long it takes us to work our way through,
the driver, the engine, the steering wheel, and the
accelerator and brake pedals, before we finally get
to the tires.

The steering wheel does not make the vehicle
change directions. The engine and the accelerator
pedal do not make it go forward. The brake pedal
does not make it stop. The **TIRES** cause the vehicle
to do all of those things.

Wait now!–Remember in the preceding chapter
when we discussed the importance of mental attitude to driving skill. If you don't, please go back and
read it again, and again and here is WHY.

If you think the steering wheel makes the car
change directions, you will always be prone to *over
using* this linkage during any driving emergency. If
you remain focused on the idea that the steering
wheel will make the car change direction; you will
use it without thought as to what your tires are doing, or if they are capable of answering a steering
demand. The same will be true of the brake pedal,
and the accelerator pedal. Worst of all, you will not
be gaining that invaluable driving experience, of

learning to understand your tires capabilities. There is information transmitted from the tires, through the linkage, to the driver. There is a tremendous amount of information coming from the tires and valuable knowledge to be gained before we ask them, to help us out of a difficult situation.

Think about the last paragraph. Ask yourselves, what you have learned or what experience you have gained from the linkages discussed. Ask the same question about the tires.

Imagine this. You are driving down the road on a wet rainy day, straining to see through the rain-splattered windshield, as the wipers beat franticly back and forth. Suddenly the car begins to hydroplane on the water covered asphalt! The car is now sliding toward the guardrail at the edge of the road!

Be honest now. What was your first instinct? Turn the steering wheel because it will make the car go away from the guardrail? Hit the brakes because they will stop the car?

Your tires had already told you they could no longer grip the pavement! Why would you still insist on asking them to make a directional change, by turning the steering wheel? Why, when they didn't immediately respond, would you insist more urgently and crank in more steering? Then when they did regain traction you had them pointed in the wrong direction and they launched your vehicle across the road into whatever was there. True case, all too often, and created one hundred percent by driver misunderstanding.

What mysterious driving trick that only the pros know do you think would solve that driving emergency? What the pros know, is first regain traction, BEFORE, you ask the tires to use it! Don't ask your tires to use traction they don't have. What the pros have, is a thorough understanding, of available tire traction. Then they put it to work! That is what we are going to do now.

Take your pencil and draw a line down the left side of your sheet of paper. This line will represent the guardrail. Now draw in the road shoulder and three driving lanes as if on a freeway or divided highway. Near the bottom of the page, draw a rectangular box to scale, representing your vehicle in the left lane. Draw in four small rectangles, representing the tires pointed straight ahead, driving down the road. This doesn't have to be a work of art. Mid way up the page, draw the vehicle again, only this time closer to the guardrail. Draw in the tires with the front tires pointed as if you were trying to steer away from the guardrail. As the vehicle slows and regains traction or bounces off the guardrail, where are the front tires going to direct it? At 55 MPH the vehicle is going to cross all three lanes and off the road to the right faster than you can correct for it. Would you like to redraw the tires and point them where they can direct the car safely?

Let's think about the brake pedal. Go back to the same scenario as before. Sliding towards the guardrail may have produced the instinct to stop, so you push on the brake pedal because it makes the car stop. It doesn't, because the tires have lost contact with the asphalt and are sliding on water like a surfboard.

Accelerator pedal? Some instincts may be to speed up to get away from the rail. Same results, tires don't have any traction right now. Please hang up and try again later.

Let's take a moment to think about what just happened. Think about our vehicle tires sliding along on top of the water. DON'T think about the guardrail. That's not where we want to be.

When the tires first started sliding, they were telling us they had lost traction, but we weren't communicating with them, because we had spent our entire driving experience communicating with the steering wheel, brake and accelerator pedals.

Now! Don't ask me, what we should have done. Ask yourself. Better yet, ask your tires. What they are going to tell you is they lost traction and they couldn't possibly have done anything more until they regained some traction.

It's your turn to talk. Go back over the scenario and then tell me, all the ways you can think of, to have gotten your tires back in touch with the asphalt. Take time to do that now. I'm listening, because I have been for years and I have been thrilled and inspired by the answers once the students began thinking about the tires.

If we are all in agreement on the importance of the tires, and the drivers ability to communicate directly with them, let's talk about what else effects this small piece of rubber in contact with the road. The actual surface area of an average car tire, in contact with the road surface, able to exercise control over the vehicle mounted above it, is smaller than the page of this book! The average adult hand, with fingers slightly spread, pressed down on a flat surface, will be close to the surface area contacted by the average car tire. That's on a clean dry road, without any other substantial forces acting on the tire.

Take another piece of paper and draw four tire surface contact areas to scale to fit the paper. You don't have to draw a perfect tread pattern, you can use squiggly lines to represent that. I do. Now keep the drawing where you can refer to it again. If you want to prove to yourselves, what your vehicle tire surface contact area actually looks like it is easy to do. Park your vehicle on a level surface as if you were going to change a tire. Get two pieces of heavy cardboard about twelve inches by twelve inches and a spray can of colored paint. I like red. Place these next to one of the tires and jack the tire up an inch off the surface. Spray paint one piece of cardboard, slip it under the tire and let the tire down. Let it set for several minutes to make a good imprint then jack it up and remove the cardboard. Use the other piece of cardboard to let the tire back down on so you don't spot the driveway. You now have an imprint of your tire surface contact area. Keep in mind this is at rest and it gets much smaller at highway speeds or when other forces are acting on it. I hope all of you will make an impression of your tire. Then hang it where you can look at it daily. Tell your friends about it. Tell them how important it is. Read your owners manual and safety warnings before jacking up the car. That will certainly be a new experience for some of you. Please note that larger taller tires will make a larger imprint than the average car tire.

For right now please put a mental picture into your brain data bank, of four pieces of rubber, about the size of your hand, holding your vehicle, you, your passengers and cargo, onto the road surface. Great! Now we go drive, with you sitting behind the wheel, above those four tires. You now have control of the tires through the steering wheel, accelerator pedal, brake pedal. That's it! Those four pieces of rubber is all there is! You are in control of this mechanical marvel we call an automobile by directing the tires! I wish it were that simple, but understanding what ultimately makes the vehicle go is only the first step. Understanding and anticipating every thing that is going to effect those four tire surface contact areas is driver control.

"Hey Mr. Advanced Driving Instructor." "Can't you just tell us how to do it?"

I could, and I will, but not necessarily the way you way you want to hear it. There are not any definitive simple single solutions to car control. That has been the problem in the past for many drivers. They don't understand why the car is doing what it is doing; therefore the response becomes a guess at best.

To help us understand the why of the automobile we need to understand clearly, as in having knowledge of, what forces are effecting the tires and what we can do to lessen the effect of these forces.

Speed—the faster you go the more the vehicle is effected by rushing air. The same effect as on an airplane wing, although vehicles are designed to not be wings and not lift, and the surface area effected by lift is reduced, it still happens. The more the lift, the less down force on the tire, the smaller the tire surface contact area!

Water—Snow—Ice—Gravel—Dirt—Grass, referred to as low traction surfaces. Does a tire have the same traction on these surfaces as it does on dry pavement?—"NO WAY!"—WHY? You can't be expected to do this or do that unless you know and understand, what you're doing. Try explaining to yourself precisely why the tires lose traction on low traction surfaces. Take some time to think about it.

Ask yourself what driving techniques, or driving judgements, need be in place to insure your tires have the traction required for you to control the car. If you are going to be driving on a low traction surface before we finish the book, please think about it as you are driving.

Vehicle weight, the direction and speed of that weight, is the predominant force acting on your vehicle tires, which the driver must understand to become skilled in car control! Vehicle weight, the direction and speed of that weight is a topic the average driver and even above average driver, for some unknown reason, does not relate to car control. Imagine putting, a three thousand-pound bowling ball, into motion at fifty-five miles per hour. Now imagine the force required to make that bowling ball turn left. An object in motion will continue in a straight line. Now don't paint me into a corner. I promised no lengthily scientific discussion. I know we all understand the "an object in motion will travel in a straight line" thing. I also know we don't apply that understanding to our automobile. Relating this to our automobile is an essential ingredient for car control. You are going to hear this repeatedly throughout the discussion. We are also going to discover WHY this is so important.

I want you to visualize looking down on the car from above. Don't look at the soft leather seats or the interior of the car. Look down on the tires. Look through the tires, to that portion of the tire in contact with the road. Stop reading for a minute, close your eyes and look with your mind.

We are going to stay up here above the car and watch the tires as we put the car through some driving maneuvers. We will put the vehicle into motion and accelerate to 30 MPH. Then we will apply the brakes gradually, as if for a stop sign. Through the brake pedal and linkage we are applying braking pressure to slow the tire but the vehicle mass wants to keep on traveling in the direction and at the speed it was traveling. It is the suspension system securely attached to the tires, which causes the vehicle to slow and ultimately stop. If not, the tires would stop but the vehicle body would keep on going. Because of this, there was some forward motion of the car body as we stopped, which the suspension absorbed. The front of the car went down and the back went up. We commonly refer to this action as weight transfer. It takes place from side to side as we turn corners; front to rear as we accelerate, and rear to front as we stop.

We all know that and have experienced it many times, so what's the big deal. The big deal is what happens to the tires! The suspension system is designed to absorb the greatest amount of this weight transfer as possible and still keep the tires firmly in contact with the road. The faster or harder we turn or stop, the greater the transfer of vehicle weight and the greater the effect on the tires.

Q: Which tire is going to have the most traction? The one with more weight pressing down on it, or the one that has the weight lifted from it by the transfer of that weight.

The tire that is lightest on the road will have from a moderate to a severe amount of traction loss, depending on the amount of weight transferred from it.

Please note that we are not going to get into a discussion of the coefficients of friction or G force loads. That might be helpful to some, but my experience has proven it does not relate to any driving action for most drivers. For this discussion, we will simply refer to those different kinds of friction, as available traction or a loss of traction.

As we increase the vehicle speed and or brake harder, in a rear wheel drive vehicle; we will see a time when the light rear tires stop rolling. The braking action on the tire exceeded the available traction between the tire and the road. We now have a skidding tire or tires.

To compensate for this, as much as possible, the brake system is proportioned so that the rear brakes can't work as hard as the front brakes. ABS, which we will discuss in detail later, helps this proportioning problem somewhat.

Front tires can also skid when the braking pressure stops the tire from rolling. In almost all cases though, when the front tires skid because of over braking, the rears are or are about to do the same. If we were driving a front wheel drive vehicle, the front tires would be most likely to skid.

A rolling tire makes the car change direction. The body of the car or the mass will always want to continue in a straight line in whatever direction it was put into motion. When excessive brake pressure is applied to the point it stops the tire from rolling, the tire "skids". It becomes a part of the vehicle mass, and goes in the direction of that mass. You can turn the steering wheel all you want and the tire can't help you because it has stopped rolling. I don't mean to sound as if I'm talking down to you because I am not. I know there are many drivers who still have not grasped this concept. They will slam on the brakes, turn the steering wheel and be shocked that the car won't change direction. Then they will turn the steering wheel more in hopes of making it change direction! If you want the tires to respond to your steering input, the tires must be rolling. The only way you will know if the tires are rolling is to stop communicating with the steering wheel and begin communicating with the tires.

There are other driving actions that effect our tire surface contact area. When we turn the vehicle, the weight is transferred in the direction we were traveling, prior to the turn and continues in that direction during the turn. This causes the body of the car to lean in that direction and the suspension system to make the adjustments to keep the tires standing up straight and pressed down onto the road surface.

Over steering and or harsh steering inputs can cause this weight to be THROWN onto the suspension and momentarily exceed it's design capability to keep the tires standing up straight and pressed firmly on the ground. The tires on the side of the car where the weight is directed can receive enough side force to cause them to distort. This can press the outside tire side wall down onto the road and lift the inside portion of that tire tread up off the road. The tires on the side opposite from where the weight was tossed may lift enough to lose that firm contact with the road.

Let's take a moment to go over what we just discussed because it has been and continues to be, an area of confusion for a lot of drivers. Understanding and anticipating weight transfer are critical parts of car control. Understanding, anticipating, weight transfer, are critical parts of car control!

To help us do this we will make another sketch. Start at the bottom right of the paper and draw a two lane road and then a left turn about half way up the page. Draw your vehicle including the four tire surface contact areas, in the right lane approaching the left turn.

The total weight and speed of the vehicle mass is traveling straight ahead. As we enter the left turn this mass wants to continue straight ahead, so draw several arrows to the outside of the turn in the direction the vehicle mass wants to go. Now move your vehicle into the middle of the turn. At this point the vehicle mass has not changed direction, so draw the arrows again, in the same direction the vehicle was traveling before entering the curve. The forces of the vehicle mass will not completely change direction, until the vehicle is again traveling in a straight line.

If this still confuses you, and I know for some it does, you will have to take my word for it. You must understand that the weight and force of vehicle mass will always travel in a straight line, in the direction it was put into motion, until a greater outside force acts on it to make it change direction. On the automobile, that outside force is the tire. Why this is so important to driver control is coming next. Please remember we stated earlier that correcting a skid is not simply turning in the direction of the skid. It is understanding and anticipating everything there is to know about a skid.

The vehicle tires made the vehicle change direction because the body, the vehicle mass, is attached to the tires by the suspension system. Otherwise the car body, vehicle mass, would have kept going straight ahead as the tires and chassis went around the corner.

With the body and it's mass still attached to the tires you can see the forces, represented by your arrows, causing the weight of the vehicle to transfer to the outside, in this case right side, of the vehicle.

Now take a moment to study your sketch and think about what is happening to each tire as the vehicle is driven around the corner. We did say each tire, because each tire is being effected differently at different points through the turn. As the vehicle first enters the corner, it is the front tires the forces are acting on and trying to pull into the right ditch. Then as the vehicle continues, the rear tires begin to receive side forces. Can you see why drivers loose control in corners? Can you anticipate which tire is most likely to break traction and when and where? If you were in the vehicle, how would each tire feel?

If the speed or harshness of the turn is sufficient, the traction between the tires and the road will be lost. That will allow the vehicle mass to continue in the direction it was headed, prior to the turn, and drag the tires in that same direction. This is commonly refered to as a skid, yet the tires were still rolling. If the rear tires break traction, it is referred to as a spin out. By looking at your sketch you can easily see why the spin out is such a difficult and dangerous loss of control for the driver.

We are going to come back to this later and more in depth as it relates to the tires and driver control techniques but we need to put some more of the ingredients together first.

If we were in a classroom I would say, "Let's take a ten minute break" and you would say "WHEW!" So would I. Please keep in mind I am in no way attempting an exact scientific explanation. I have tried that before and it has not worked for most students. What I have found to be the most effective explanation is what we are doing.

Another common area of communication failure between driver and tire, is inflation pressure. It is the correct tire pressure inside the tire that keeps the tire sidewall rigid and the tread pattern working to design specifications. Now that we have a good grasp of how weight and side force effects our tire contact surface area let's think about an under-inflated tire. It doesn't have to be a great amount to seriously effect car control, not to mention tire life. Go back to the prior sketch when we talked about the effect of weight transfer. Now suppose the right front tire is under-inflated, with a weakened side wall and a not so solid tread contact area! Can you visualize how it rolls under as you enter the turn? Can you imagine how that is going to feel through the steering wheel as the right front of the car plows straight ahead instead of turning left? Do you honestly want to gamble on an under-inflated tire performing well going around a corner or during the driving emergency? Traveling in a straight line or at low speeds you may not feel any difference in that tire. The moment you transfer weight to that tire or ask it to do some work, you will feel it 'plow' and it may make a kind of slight squealing sound.

Let's say you leave home in the morning and making the first right turn the vehicle feels normal. The next turn you make is a left turn and the vehicle responds sluggishly and you find yourself increasing the steering to get around the turn. What would you suspect to be the problem? I would suspect the right front tire was low on air and I would check it as soon as I safely could. I definitely would not wait to check it the next time I stopped for fuel. If a rear tire is low, it will cause the rear of the vehicle to sway or feel squirmy when weight is transferred to that tire.

There have been numerous cases of drivers replacing vehicle shocks or struts, when the problem was low tire pressure. If you are driving and you begin to feel unusual vibrations or swaying, or the steering feels heavier than normal slow down and pull over as soon as you safely can and check your tires. If while coming to a stop, the vehicle pulls slightly to the right or left, check that tire. If you absolutely must drive on a low tire reduce speed and reduce speed to a crawl while turning where weight is transferred to the low tire. If you have driven on a low tire, have the tire removed from the rim and the inside of the tire side wall inspected. It may look fine on the outside while the inside is seriously damaged.

After conducting low tire demonstrations with a large group of students, it is not unusual to find a handful or more of ground up rubber inside the tire. Two days ago I asked a group of twelve students when was the last time they had checked their tires. Five had not checked tire pressure in over three months. Two had never checked tire pressure because their cars weren't even a year old yet.

When was the last time you checked your vehicle tires for correct inflation pressure? When was the last time you read your owners manual?

Cold inflation pressure doesn't mean, wait for winter. Check your pressure after the vehicle has been parked overnight. A short drive to the nearest air station will not substantially increase pressure to a point of being inaccurate. If you are on a long trip and you suspect a tire is low, check it! As a rule, hot inflation pressure will read four PSI higher. Therefore, if the cold inflation pressure was supposed to be, thirty and the hot inflation pressure read thirty, you were correct; the tire is four PSI under-inflated.

The four-PSI is a good general rule, but it may not apply to all tires or all vehicles so check your owners manual.

I would like all of you to think about this. An accurate tire gage costs less than a fast food lunch and is as readily available.

We are making good progress at understanding the ingredients and putting the recipe together. We know how even an experienced driver can suddenly freeze up. We have a better mental picture of our tires actual surface area contact. How vehicle speed, road conditions, correct inflation pressure, steering input and weight transfer will effect those four pieces of rubber.

By understanding this we can think about our driving habits and better evaluate if some of these habits need to be corrected or modified. We can also begin to predict what the vehicle is going to do, before we input a demand the tires can't answer. We will continue to put it together until the puzzle is completed.

Chapter Four

YOUR MIND SET ABOUT CAR CONTROL.

Please remember we are using a building block approach and there are a number of ingredients, which go into the car control recipe.

Let's imagine this. We are driving around a sharp left corner at highway speed. The weight is being transferred to the right side tires, but the suspension is doing the job and keeping the right side tires in contact with the road. The left side tires are lighter than if the vehicle was traveling straight ahead, but they are also maintaining good contact.

Get a good mental picture of the four tire contact areas and the forces acting on them! Refer to your sketch if you need to, but then do it again mentally with your eyes closed.

File it away and insure it remains on the mental disc. Because now we are going to create a driving emergency and our understanding of those four tire contact areas will be a vital source of information as to WHAT we should direct our vehicle to do.

Suddenly there is a vehicle coming head on at us in our lane of travel! DON'T LOOK AT THAT VE-HICLE! THAT IS NOT WHERE WE WANT TO BE!

If we jerk the steering wheel to the left how are the tires going to react? The right side tires were heavily loaded going around the corner and the left side tires were light. Do we want to throw more weight on the right side tires and take more weight off the left side tires while turning the front tires more, all at the same time? Do we want to jerk our foot off the accelerator, which will cause more weight to transfer to the front tires and lift the rear tires more? Do we want to jam on the brakes and become a passenger? Do we want to turn right and drive off the road into the ditch, the trees, whatever?

I can not honestly tell you what I would do. I can tell you I would not take the head on! We will discuss this more later.

We could certainly build on this scenario by add-ing what the other car was or was not doing, but that would not be the point. The vital point here is to continue to drive our car and to have the under-standing to NOT make some arbitrary demand on our vehicle that the tires can't possibly support.

Let's back up and re-enter that exact same cor-ner, only this time, we see a vehicle stopped in our lane of travel and traffic approaching in the oncom-ing lane! There is not enough room between the stopped vehicle and the guard rail to get by on the right! There might be enough room to get stopped in time!

Q: You are on the brakes hard, as you should be, and your vehicle does not have ABS. What do you

expect your vehicle to do if you brake too hard? That is, hard enough to stop a tire or tires from rolling and begin skidding.

Think what your tires are doing at this time. Refer back to your left turn sketch. Driving around the left corner, weight is transferred to the right side of the car. As you apply the brakes, weight is being transferred forward. The front of your car is going down and the rear is coming up! The right front tire has the most weight on it and is doing the most work. Which tire has the least weight on it and doing the least work?—Don't say spare tire!—Say left rear tire.

Depending on the vehicle you are driving, either the right front or the left rear is most likely to skid first. If the rear tire skids, the back of the car will begin to rotate to the right in the direction of the weight transfer. If the right front tire skids, the front of the car will lose steering traction and begin skidding straight ahead, which in a left hand corner means toward the guardrail on the right.

Q: Front, rear, right, left, whichever— whatever! What should you do?

Continue to drive your car! If pressing on the brakes too hard caused a tire or tires to skid, don't push so hard on the brake pedal. Lift off the pedal enough to get the tire or tires rolling again, and continue to drive the car, and continue to brake hard. You need to get your car stopped, or at least slowed enough to lessen the impact if you can't completely stop, because the scenario gives you no place to escape.

"How hard should I push?"

Ask your tires; stay in close communication with them; keep them rolling.

Right about now, we have a serious discussion going, and some of the things you are saying, are not pretty! That's fine. This is a discussion and I want you to think and question, and think and question, until you have the answers.

Remember, this is a 'how you can book', not a 'how to book'.

If you were driving in a straight line, you would have all your tires' available traction to stop. Road conditions being good, I'd probably say "stand on those brakes, and be ready to let up if a tire skids!" However, you were going around a corner, with an undetermined amount of traction loss at the inside tires and additional traction demand on the outside tires due to weight transfer and cornering, with oncoming traffic and no room for error.

The instinctive reaction of the average driver would be to 'slam on the brakes'! With what you know now, do you think that would be a good idea? You certainly need to be doing some serious braking, but you don't have room to fix a bad skid!

How hard should you press the pedal is going to come from what you understood about traction and weight transfer, and their combined effect on your tires, before and after, you went into the corner. Now that you are into the situation, you have to talk to your tires. Keep them rolling and pointed where you want to go. That is NOT into the oncoming traffic!

We can paint all kinds of, 'what ifs', and 'buts', into the two scenarios I have given you. We can arrange them into any number of probable solutions, but before we do that, I want you to think about this.

What is the outcome likely to be if you go driving into that corner, without any idea or understanding of what your vehicle is capable of, or why?

You don't have to answer that question. The crash statistics have answered it for you.

Up to now we have kept our focus on those physical things that a mentally prepared driver should be able to control. Now, let's look at a mental thing that a mentally prepared driver MUST control.

To do this we are going to revisit the first scenario. You are driving around a sharp left corner, when suddenly, there is a vehicle coming at you in your lane of travel.

Remember the startle thing? Well please believe it, because the instant you see that vehicle coming at you, you are going to get a great big load of those body chemicals dumped into your system! If you don't fix it right now, they are going to keep on entering your system and tightening your muscles until you can't move!

This startle isn't caused by your sense of hearing. It is being caused by your sense of sight. Plugging your ears won't help. Moving your eyes will! Moving your eyes will! Looking away from that which is frightening you and about to cause panic will help. It will give you an escape option and put the muscles to work for you.

Earlier I told you don't look at that car! That's not where you want to be! I put it in capital letters because that is not where you want to be, but it is where you will be, if you focus on it!

If you focus on, stare at, that onrushing car about to smash into you, what information is your sense of sight communicating to your brain! Hopeless information with no way out! By continuing to focus on the other car you are limiting what options your sense of sight is giving your brain!

Under this condition, your only option is to 'STOP'!—Your foot is going to jam down on the brake pedal so hard all four tires are going to stop rolling and start skidding! Even if you understand you must get off the brakes, to get the tires rolling, to regain control of your car; your muscles aren't going to let you because they have locked up tight. 'WHY'? Because your eyes are transmitting information to your brain that something terrible is about to happen to you and the body chemicals are flooding the system without any options! If you are driving an Anti-skid Braking System equipped car, the tires won't stop rolling and skid, but they are still pointed in the direction you are looking; straight ahead at the oncoming car.

TURN AWAY!-Just maybe, and this is slim, you didn't jam on the brakes and skid the tires, so they can respond to you're steering input, or you have an ABS equipped car, but where are you looking! At something you are desperately trying to avoid! Your body is going to react accordingly and your hands are going to spin the steering wheel as fast as they can, away from the impending disaster; breaking traction by excessive steering input or redirecting the car into another obstacle. If you want to drive around the oncoming vehicle, you are going to have to look where you want to drive and then the steering input will be precise and controlled. Even ABS can't help you if you are grossly over steering and throwing the weight of the vehicle from side to side. **If you want to drive around the oncoming vehicle, you MUST LOOK where you want to go.**

Q. What should you do?

Continue to drive your automobile! Look where you want to go! Use your steering wheel, brake pedal, accelerator pedal, as required to insure, your tires can take you in that direction!

"What if I look in a direction my tires can't take me?"

CRASH!—However, I didn't say your options were limited to a single direction. Look for something else! Don't ever give up! Continue to drive your automobile! Even to the point of impact and beyond! If that is your only option, then, *pick the point of impact*, by looking at it and driving through it! IF,–That is your only option.

Proper control and use of the eyes is a major ingredient, to all aspects of car control. While driving, our eyes are the primary information and sensory input source. When I said control of your eyes, I meant that. Looking away from something is not a natural reaction, looking and staring at it is. You will have to tell your eyes where to look and you will have to understand and believe how critical it is to accomplish that, because it won't happen naturally.

For me to accomplish my part of this discussion; which is to make sure you understand and believe; let's talk about this some more. If I were only allowed to tell you one thing about driving; proper use of the eyes would be it.

What if some other driver runs a red light and suddenly that vehicle is broadside to you in the intersection!

How much steering input does it take to drive around that car? Not any amount that any of us can't quickly input! Why then, does driving around that car, happen so infrequently during this type of driving emergency? I hope you know the answer to that one by now.

The moment you saw that car, one hundred percent of your attention was focused on it! I think that is natural and is going to happen, in that first fraction of a second, but if you allow your attention to stay focused on that car, who is attending to driving your car?

None of us has any serious problem driving where we are looking. We will all have serious problems trying to drive where we are not looking. Another example of eye control is crossing a narrow bridge or driving through construction zones with reduced lane width and huge concrete barriers on either side. If we will continue to look down the road, we will manage these areas correctly. It is when we glance to the right or left to see how close we are that the hands get jerky and we run the risk of colliding with something.

Let's revisit the intersection scenario and let's say there simply isn't any place to take our car. How we use our eyes is still critical. If you can't possibly avoid the collision where do you want your car to impact that car?

Into the driver or passenger side door, commonly referred to as a "T–Bone crash", or towards the rear or the front? We should try to drive away from the motion of the other vehicle whenever possible. If the vehicle is crossing from your right to your left, turning right will be your best chance to avoid that vehicles forward motion. Turning left will take you in the direction of the other vehicle's forward motion. Striking the center of the other car is the worst possible option. Striking the rear or front will result in spinning the other vehicle and reduce the force of the impact. However, do you think you are going to do anything, if you don't make your eyes give your brain some options?

The point I want to make, is the difference between driving around something, as opposed to driving away from it. If you are trying to drive around something, you are looking where you intend to drive. If you arc wildly trying to drive away from it, you are looking at it and your chances of colliding with it or something else are increased.

When you are pulling into your driveway at home, you don't keep looking down the street, trying to guess where the driveway is. You look at it, you input steering, you correct the steering input if necessary, and you drive.

If you are focused, staring, at something blocking your path of travel, your steering input, at best, is going to be a blind guess! Add the startle effect on your muscles and it is going to be a wild blind guess!

Do you want to drive into the big tree or the small tree? I know.—Neither one! A preconceived mind-set that eliminates necessary options is a dangerous mind-set. Do you want to drive into the head on collision or into the ditch? Do you want to drive into the back of the car in front of you, or the parking meter post?

Watch out for those big concrete and steel light poles,—they hurt!

Have you ever wondered why automobiles collide with power poles along the highway? Think about this for a moment. A pole occupies how much space, compared to space that is around it? I can not say for an absolute fact, so I won't, but guess where the driver who ran into the power pole was looking!

Every experienced advanced driving instructor I have known can tell you where the student driver is looking, by observing how he or she is reacting physically. If they are looking at the traffic cones, they will over steer and over brake, frequently both, at the same time. If they are focused on where they intend to drive, the steering is smooth and precise. The braking may be rough, but not the steering. Erratic steering is caused by the blind guess syndrome. Rough or awkward steering is another problem.

"Not another ingredient!"

I know you are getting fidgety. We have already covered a lot of good information. You understand it, and you're ready for that recipe. I wish it were that easy. If it were, the numbers of the fatalities and serious injuries on our highways would not be what they are today.

Stay with me awhile, because we are not there yet. We understand what can cause a driver to freeze up and how to avoid that happening to us! We know how to anticipate and understand available traction. We know how to communicate with our tires. We know how to manage our tires through the linkages inside the vehicle during the driving emergency, and we know how important our eyes are to car control. What more can there be?

Not much, only all those things which create driving problems and all those things that can effectively negate other driving skills and all the methodology that puts it together to complete the driver. That's all, not much.

With that said, this brings us to another bad driving habit that causes serious problems during the driving emergency.

Managing the steering wheel, with your hands properly placed on the wheel, is not something the majority of you do well.

I know you have heard all this before and totally ignore it, because you are convinced it makes no difference. Under normal driving conditions you must be correct, because you are driving with one hand, or with the palm on the wheel or the wrist or one finger and are managing just fine. At least you think you are. However, take a moment to think about what we have already discussed. During those moments of high excitation, with or without the startle effect, your muscles are receiving an extra dose of chemicals and they are going to respond a great deal more aggressively, than when you are relaxed.

To make this point in the past I have asked students to drive around the course slowly with their hands wherever they choose. They do just fine. Then I ask them to drive between 35 and 45 MPH. Difficulties begin to arise in the confined space, quick reaction drill areas. Then we go into the driving drills at highway speeds with cones rushing at them and me yelling instructions. The drivers reactions go from mild to wild! Muscle control?—Imagine if the cones were other automobiles!

I advocate proper steering wheel management as a tool to make you a better driver under all conditions, and to enhance your driving attitude and mindset. Correct steering wheel management is an essential life saving tool; during the driving emergency or when road conditions dictate a greater degree of precise control.

Proper hand management will prevent you from over steering, or jerking the wheel or getting your arms all crossed up at the worst possible moment.

Two hands are better than one! I personally am not hung up on the clock face 9 and 3 or 10 and 2 hand positions on the wheel. I have been wearing a digital watch for so long I forget where those positions are anyway.

Some highway safety experts now advocate, placing the hands, on the lower portion of the steering wheel, because of burns caused when the air bags have deployed. I'm a bit dubious on that one, especially if it creates a car control problem for the driver, which then leads to a crash where the air bag will deploy.

Here again, it is not going to help for me to tell you where to place your hands on the wheel, any more than it did when you heard it or read it from other sources. This you can believe! Improper steering wheel control, is improper tire control, and improper tire control is a crash waiting to happen!

For proper steering wheel management, this is what you should be able to do. With both hands on the wheel, move the tires from pointing straight ahead, to maximum left turn and to maximum right turn, while keeping both hands on wheel at all times. With both hands on the wheel, at all times, make quick steering changes, in both directions, without crossing your arms, or getting your elbows blocked by your body or interior of the car. When you can do that, you will have mastered the technique of shuffle, or push pull, or whatever anyone wishes to call it, steering. Read the explanation of what you should be able to do again. You will realize, to do that, your hands can't be close together, they can't go hand over hand and they will have to be positioned in proportion to your body. Don't get frustrated. It is not something you will master in an hour or a day. You will have to practice and practice.

Do this while the vehicle is parked, with the parking brake set, and the engine running so you have power assist steering and you can feel the tires. Don't do this inside a garage with the engine running. Sit behind the wheel of your car and practice until you find the hand and arm positions that allow for the above. You will be very close to what most experts would tell you to do. Keeping in mind if you are gripping the steering wheel too tightly now, you are going to squeeze it to death during moments of extreme excitement.

Practice this technique until it becomes as natural for your muscles as blinking or breathing. Then you will drive that way. You will have gained invaluable experience about car control during the driving emergency, without having to pay a big price to discover you wished you had known that before.

Another problem area I have notice with most drivers is how they apply the brakes. Picking your foot up and placing it on the brake pedal may seem quit natural but you are using big muscles. What happens to our muscles during moments of extreme excitation or startle? Probably where the phrase "slam on the brakes" came from. Because that's what's going to happen when the chemicals hit the system and those muscles become coiled springs looking for release.

Another concern with your leg up in the air and whole foot on the pedal is what if you need to get off the brakes or perhaps lessen the braking effect with those big muscles jammed down on the pedal!

Could our brake pedal control be best accomplished by using the toe portion of the foot on the brake pedal and keeping the heel in contact with the floor? Should we ever, "slam" on the brakes? You know what that is going to do to your tires and weight transfer.

Try this, pick your foot up and "slam" on that imaginary brake pedal! Tighten your leg muscles, push hard, even harder! Now lift your foot up off that pedal! A bit shaky, maybe some hesitation, most certainly gross movement!

This time keep your heel on the floor with the toe angled towards the accelerator, then quickly rotate the toe portion and apply the brakes aggressively, push harder, now lift the toe portion of your foot off the brake pedal. Any problems? I didn't think so. Practice this until it becomes, at least somewhat comfortable before driving, then continue to practice until it becomes natural. Those of you with small feet may have to pick your foot up, but still use the toe portion and rotate to the brake pedal, instead of lifting up and slamming down.

A somewhat intangible, although real benefit, of correct hand, foot, and body control, is the calming effect of precise sure muscle movement, during the driving emergency.

We are certainly not going to go driving with the intention of getting involved in a driving emergency so we can gain experience! Yet, unless we understand and practice, correct driver control techniques, that is exactly what we are doing, albeit unintentional!

Chapter Five

ANTICIPATORY DRIVING

We have discussed a considerable amount of the "Why" you should do certain things behind the wheel and some limited, 'How' you should do them. With this understanding and appreciation of what car control is all about we need to talk about a driving skill that is equally as important as defensive driving skill.

Anticipatory driving skill, is an integral part, of defensive driving skill. It is also an essential requirement for all levels, of driver skill development, from inexperienced to professional.

The human body was not designed to travel at the speeds that modern day automobiles and roads take us to. If it had been, we would have the eyes and reflexes of a hawk! We do not. Therefore, we must use our minds to the greatest extent possible to make up for those deficiencies.

That is called 'Anticipation' of what is about to happen. At highway speeds it has already happened before we have time to think through a process of reaction.

As logical and simplistic as this is, it's still widely misunderstood and seldom practiced by the average driver. A major reason is the lack of understanding about all aspects of car control. How can you anticipate something you don't know exists? How can you anticipate a skid if you don't understand what actually causes one? How can you anticipate a loss of traction if you don't understand your tires, or weight transfer?

Had we discussed anticipatory driving in Chapter One, it would have been a waste of time and summarily dismissed by most of you. I wouldn't blame you, because there would have been nothing to associate it to. Unfortunately, the same thing has happened to most of the valuable defensive driving information you have received, and continue to receive. I think by the time we finish, we will have gained a much better understanding of the 'WHY' defensive driving is important. We will have something to relate it to besides statistical data that tells us one out of so many is going to be seriously injured. The average driver doesn't relate to numbers because the numbers aren't hurting us.

Since we now have an understanding of anticipatory driving, let's go back and drive the sharp left corner. As we approach the corner this time, we look for the warning sign, with the arrow indicating the degree of the turn and the speed in MPH. If the sign is not there, we look to see how sharp the corner is by judging how far through the corner we can see and begin to slow the vehicle accordingly.

We are not anticipating, a head on collision, or a stopped vehicle, every time we go around a corner! If we were, we would never go around a corner! What we are anticipating, is how our vehicle is going to react as we make the turn. How are our tires going to grip the surface? How much traction will we have, to deal with ANY emergency? It may be nothing more than debris or water on the road surface that will cause the right front tire to lose traction and we are headed for the ditch. However, because we understand what is going to happen when that right front tire crosses that low traction area, we anticipate, and slow quickly, and or drive around the low traction spot.

At the beginning of the book, we asked how the driver was supposed to gain experience, about the driving emergency, without going out and getting in a wreck! Anticipatory driving is an essential part of the process.

Each time you drive around a corner, learn something from that experience. How does your vehicle feel? In which direction is the weight being transferred and to which tire? How do your tires feel? How much traction do you have? How far ahead can you see? Could you stop quickly if you needed to? Could you accelerate quickly if you needed to? If a driving emergency suddenly occurred, could you and your vehicle handle it? Anticipate that someday it could happen and begin to make the car control adjustments to your driving habits NOW!

If you find yourself continually on the brakes as you drive through a corner you are either uncertain about the available traction or are in the habit of entering the corner slightly faster than you should. Let me pose a couple of questions to you about driving around corners or making sharp turns.

What is the driving penalty for entering a corner or negotiating a sharp turn too slowly? A redundant question, of course.

What is the driving penalty for entering a corner or negotiating a sharp turn too fast? Not at all redundant is it? Take a quiet moment or two to think about those questions. Take time during driving to ask yourself those questions as you are approaching any corner or sharp turn situation.

What is the driving response to entering a corner too fast? "OH—NO"

What is the driving response to entering a corner too slow? Pleasantly unlimited!

Let me give you a hypothetical situation. Suppose you and I, are driving identical vehicles. Suppose we have a road with a 55 MPH speed limit and we select a corner on that road which is negotiable at a maximum speed of 45 MPH for our vehicles.

Suppose you enter the corner at 40 MPH, (5 MPH slower than possible). You drive smoothly through the beginning of the corner until you can see safely down the road, and then accelerate back to 55 MPH, as you leave the corner.

Suppose I enter the same corner at 50 MPH, (5 MPH faster than possible). I realize my mistake and somehow miraculously manage, through great driving skill, to brake and turn and reduce speed enough to cling to the road at 45 MPH, as I leave the corner.

Which one of us would have negotiated the corner the fastest? You would have!

Which one of us would have negotiated the corner the safest? You would have! It might be a good idea if you read that paragraph again. It might be a great idea if you keep it in the back of your mind and think of it every time you approach a corner.

The moral of this story; we can gain valuable driving experience by understanding some basic driving principals. We don't have to guess and take chances and crash to gain driving experience.

We all know that intersections are the most likely place for a crash to occur, yet we don't anticipate it ever happening to us! Therefore, we spend our driving life without gaining any experience about intersections!

"Wait a minute!—If I have a green light or am on a through street, I'm supposed to slow down for every intersection?"

I didn't say that, and I don't necessarily advocate it, simply because you may become a problem for other drivers. If it didn't effect other drivers, I might ask you what would be so bad about that.

What I want to do is ask you a question. As we approach an intersection, where is the information, about any possible hazards, going to come from, and how are you going to collect it?

Good for you! You got it! Look around! Take your eyes off the light, if it goes yellow, your peripheral vision will pick it up. Anticipate! If you ever get startled by other drivers actions at any intersection, shame on you! An unexpected driving emergency, happening to the complete driver, at or near an intersection? 'NO Way'! A driving emergency, perhaps.

Your eyes are your only source of information here. Use them and make that action a driving habit until it happens automatically; then you will be gaining experience every time you approach or cross an intersection.

'Why' it is so important to make looking around an unconscious habit and practice it repeatedly, is because of another habit. I call it eye numb. That is when we wander off, mentally. Our eyes are still sending information to the brain, but it is blurry information, because we are staring straight ahead into space seeing nothing. During that time, we may be driving the car, but we are not in control of it, nor our road surface. Anticipate, and by doing so your eyes will be in search of information because you told them to be.

Try day dreaming, or going deep into thought, when your eyes are constantly moving, searching, seeing and sending different images to the brain.

Anticipatory driving skills are also used in subtle ways. You are preparing to enter a limited access roadway and are approaching the acceleration lane, but the driver in front of you is slowing instead of speeding up.

What do you anticipate that driver is going to do? You're correct again. It happens frequently. That driver is going to slow and wait for an opening in traffic instead of accelerating to highway speed and merging in.

If you anticipated this action, why would you follow and put yourself into the same situation? Why not hesitate, until the acceleration lane is clear, and then use the acceleration lane for what it was intended? Why put yourself into a potentially dangerous driving situation when you are capable of anticipating the outcome?

You are capable of developing and using anticipatory driving skills if you choose to do so! I hope I am capable of demonstrating to you, through our conversation, WHY you must, if you intend to become a complete driver.

If we insist on practicing reactionary driving skills, we will constantly find ourselves in situations where we are reacting! What experience are we gaining from reactionary driving?

We are all going to have to react to driving situations from time to time. There is no dispute about that. My point is; would you prefer to be driving your vehicle knowing what is about to happen, or would you rather wait until the vehicle tells you it is happening? Would you prefer to be reacting *AS* the situation develops, or *AFTER* the situation develops? That is the difference between anticipatory driving and reactionary driving. You decide!

Chapter Six

THE "HOW"

Q: While driving in heavy traffic how do you avoid a vehicle, suddenly stopped in front of you?

"Slam on the brakes and hope for the best because that is all you can do in heavy traffic?"

You may not be able to avoid the vehicle suddenly stopped in front of you!

What did you want me to say?

If you were following too closely, or if you didn't see what the driver in front of you was about to respond to, or if any number of other 'ifs', you are in a difficult situation. I didn't say hopeless. What other options do you have, other than slamming into the car stopped in front of you? What car control techniques will need to be applied for those options to work?

Before we get into the how of this situation, let's take some time to understand the why. The instant you realized that vehicle was stopping directly in your path your foot is coming off the accelerator and going for the brake pedal. You may be looking frantically for an escape route. You may be turning the steering wheel to drive around the stopped vehicle. Any or all of those actions are going to be triggered by what your eyes are telling your mind and by what your driving instincts have become up to that point in time. If your foot went onto the brake pedal and tried to push it through the floor your eyes were fixated on the taillights of the stopped vehicle and stopping was your only option. It may be your only option, but don't look at the trunk of the other car because that is not where you want to be stopped. You have made an instinctive decision and acted upon it but this situation is not over yet. You may or may not have made the right decision but it has been done. What matters most now, is what you do next. Put your eyes to work and glance around quickly. Give your other senses a chance to be heard. You need to be feeling what the tires are doing and you need to be listening to what they are saying. At highway speeds, the entire situation could change in less than one second. An escape route may suddenly be available. The vehicle behind may be about to slam into you. Continue to drive your vehicle. The average driver commits to an initial response. Whatever comes after that is without thought or focus. This is not a blatant criticism on my part because I know the average driver has been told what to do and how to do it but when that is insufficient, there isn't any thing else in the data bank. Let's put something else into our data banks.

How many different car control actions do you think you are capable of in two seconds? Can you go

from accelerator to brake, from looking at one object to scanning right and left and behind, from steering straight ahead to steering around something,
from hard braking to soft braking while steering
around something? Why don't you sit in your vehicle
while it is safely parked with the engine running and
find out. Imagine the car suddenly stopped in front
of you! Rotate the toe portion of your foot from the
accelerator to the brake pedal and apply maximum
effect pressure while looking for an escape route and
checking behind. Be prepared to ease off the brakes
if a tire skids. If you find an escape route, ease up on
the brake as you input steering so the tires have traction for the steering demand. Imagine hard braking
as the weight is transferred and you're pressed
against the seat belt and the front of the car dives
downward. Imagine jerking your foot off the pedal
and the car rebounding upwards and lifting the front
tires and regaining speed while you are trying to turn.
Don't imagine; pay close attention when I said EASE
off the brake pedal. That doesn't mean slowly. That
means incrementally so you keep the vehicle weight
pressed down on the front tires while giving some of
the braking traction demand to the steering traction demand. Practice being hard on the brakes and
easing up to make a steering input but the car doesn't
change direction instantly. Resist the instinct to add
more steering. You input the correct amount you
just didn't let up on the brakes enough. If you are
driving an ABS equipped vehicle and the ABS is functioning correctly the easing up on the brakes won't
be required because the system will be doing that
for you. You will feel it through the brake pedal and
you will feel the tires rolling so all you need to do is

stay hard on the brakes and focus on the steering requirements.

What if you found out there was a state of the art driving simulator in a local area and every one could use it with no lines and no waiting at their convenience? Would you go? Will you at least take the time to practice on your own vehicle?

I personally would be pleased to no end if I could find a way to allow every driver to experience a day of advanced driver training. I can't, and as hard as we may work towards that goal, it won't happen soon. What we can do is what we are doing now. If we take a few minutes each day to improve our driving skills, we might be amazed at what we stand to gain.

Why don't you practice the two-second simulation, each time you get behind the wheel, before you put the vehicle into motion? What are a few seconds out of your day worth? What possible improvements can it create as you embark on the most dangerous activity the average person does on a daily basis? If nothing else, it may help to remind you what it is you are about to go do.

It is actually very common, for even experienced drivers, to be uncertain about how hard to apply the brakes during a driving emergency. I have talked with many students who have been driving an ABS equipped car for several years and have never experienced the ABS. This is completely understandable, but it creates problems if the driving emergency should arise.

How hard can you apply the brakes and still keep the tires rolling, is a difficult question for many drivers, so let's at least take the mystery out of that problem.

There is a significant difference between how quickly an action occurs and how much force is applied. Maximum effective braking is accomplished quickly not forcefully. That is another reason we rotate the toe portion of our foot to the brake pedal as opposed to lifting our leg and thrusting the foot downward. We are attempting to apply maximum allowable pressure on the brake pedal as quickly as we can, not as forcefully as we can. The tires are the recipients of the braking application so ask the question quickly and be prepared to respond to the answer as quickly. If you are certain of the outcome, you can make a demand. If you are uncertain, you will have to ask the questions. The tires will answer immediately in either case. Don't be timid about asking the question.

"But what if we push too hard, and stop the tire, and begin to skid?"

You received the answer from the tires you were waiting for. Fix the skid

"That's great, but I'm not so sure I understand their language!"

Oh—that's right, you haven't had the opportunity to talk to your tires during a crisis. Well,— like us when they get excited they talk fast, and it really helps if you have taken the time to understand them. A rolling tire sends consistent vibrations through the steering wheel and through the vehicle in general. It emits a soft soothing humming sound. It bumps and burps if you drive it through a pot hole in the road and it shimmies if it is out of balance or alignment. It complains if it is low on air and tends to resist whatever you ask it to do and has a tendency to lay down on the job. Otherwise, happy tires just kind of hum along, but like us, they seriously object to being forced to do something they can not do.

During your request to stop the car quickly, they will alert you by emitting a chirping sound as the happy hum turns to a stutter. They will let you know how hard they are working by how much weight is being transferred onto them. If you feel like the vehicle is about to be brought to a halt but it is still traveling fast forward the tires are telling you they have done all they can! If you didn't feel or hear that, the next thing they will do is scream in a steady wail and cease transmitting vibrations as they begin sliding down the road. You are now in a skid and you will have to let the tires roll if you want to regain control of your automobile.

"But how much should we lift off the brake pedal?" "If we lift completely off we're not stopping at all!"

You just answered your question. Lift until you get the tire rolling again while keeping the front of the car down and the weight on the front tires. Then apply pressure again, not quite so hard, and continue to apply brake pedal pressure. As the vehicle mass slows, the tires gain traction. The forces pushing the tires down the road are being reduced and the suspension system has absorbed and distributed the initial weight transfer so there is more traction for added braking until you come to a complete stop.

Communicate with your tires. If your only option is to stop, then the tires and weight transfer are your only sources of information.

If you have never taken the time to communicate with your tires and suspension system, don't wait for the driving emergency. Start now. You may be suprised how easy it is and how much they have to tell you.

An important point, that can not be overstressed, is that the condition of the road surface has to be anticipated, prior to emergency braking!

On a slippery road surface, a skidding tire will slide faster and farther, than it will on a clean dry road surface! It is also more difficult to get the tire rolling again because the traction between the tire and the road is greatly reduced! Understanding this is critically important! It is also a subject widely mis-understood.

To help us understand, let's do this. Imagine tak-ing a round object about a foot or so in diameter and an inch thick. A small wheel, if you will. Stand it up straight on a table or counter top and place your hands near the top of the wheel, one on each side, and push your hands together to hold the wheel. Now roll the wheel along keeping your hands near the top. It doesn't take much pressure from your hands to stop the wheel and it isn't difficult to re-lease the pressure and get the wheel rolling again. Now imagine making the counter top slippery and try rolling your wheel along. The slightest pressure from your hands will stop it rolling and you will al-most have to let go completely to get it rolling again.

That is how your vehicle disc brakes work. How they are mounted to your vehicle wheels is a great deal more complicated and of no significant impor-tance to this discussion. When you push on the brake pedal, it is like pushing your hands together. You can slow the wheel. You can stop the wheel. You can release pressure and let the wheel roll again. On a slippery surface, stopping the wheel is easy, getting it rolling again is a great deal more difficult. ABS is of tremendous assistance here, and we will discuss this system soon.

Please be aware, that on a slippery road surface, even an experienced, highly skilled driver is going to need additional space to get the tire rolling again after a skid. If the tires were turned sharply to the right or left, they may have to be pointed straight ahead again to get them rolling. Perhaps this will convince us to adjust our driving habits.

The reason skid control is such a hot topic can be easily stated. Every driver wants to discover the secret to controlling the vehicle in this situation. The secret is, don't get in that situation.

Within the community of advanced driving instructors, skid control on slippery surfaces is referred to as a perishable skill. The best of us will not get it right every time, where spaces to maneuver is limited to that of a public street. This skill also requires continual practice to maintain that skill level. What we do know for absolute certainty. Don't get there to start with! Most of you don't want to hear that, and we will talk more about this later.

Slamming on the brakes and hoping for the best, is NOT where you want to be. It is not where you should be. It is not where you have to be!

There is more to discuss about proper emergency braking technique. HOWEVER—ONE MORE TIME— That has to be done PRIOR, to the emergency. During those split seconds, there will not be time to analyze: The condition of your tires. The condition of the road surface. The stopping distance required for different road surfaces. The position of your foot on the brake pedal. The driveability, (that's my word) of an escape route. The position of your hands on the steering wheel. How your ABS is going to work.

Before we put our automobile into motion, we must know the condition of the tires. If your tires are worn out, not much tread left, or unevenly worn, or under inflated, how are they going to respond, to any given driving situation?

"Hey—Come on!" "My tires may be worn but they passed inspection and I can't afford new tires this month!"

I can't either, but I know and understand how the condition of my tires effects their performance. I can afford to alter my driving habits accordingly.

Why do tires have treads? That is, why aren't they smooth, like racing tires?

Why do sanctioning officials halt racing if it rains?—In fact, some sanctioned motor sports do race in the rain, but not on slick tires.

The tire tread allows the tire to displace water and debris and still maintain contact with the road surface to the design specifications of the tire manufacturer. The tread also allows the tire to grip surfaces such as snow, dirt, and mud.

If you are driving, on tires that just did pass the last inspection, with not much visible tire tread, how do you expect them to react on wet, muddy, or snow covered surfaces?—Do you think you should allow for the fact that you have limited traction at best under those conditions?

I can certainly understand not having the means or desire to replace your tires until you must. Been there myself.

I can not understand nor accept, endangering your life and the lives of others, by driving on improperly inflated tires! Nor on nearly worn out tires, as if they were in excellent condition!

When was it you said you last had a good chat with your tires to see how they were doing?

During one of our earlier conversations, I stated that the complete driver was also in control of the road surface being driven on. I meant that sincerely. There is nothing complicated for any of us about anticipating and predicting the traction available due to changing road surface conditions. There is something extremely complicated about waiting to do it during the driving emergency!

Frequently, I have asked groups of students, "Do you have the same traction on a wet road surface as you have on a dry road surface?" They all know the answer, and so do you.

"So what is the point?" The point is I want them, and you, to ask yourselves the same question prior to driving whenever the surface condition changes. Ask the question in relation to your vehicle and tires. The best tires on the market today will require some driver anticipated driving adjustments. If your tires are far from the best, they will require even more driving adjustments.

Some areas or sections of the road may also require additional anticipation and driving adjustment. For example, the surface within multiple car lengths of any major intersection is going to be effected by the numbers of vehicles that stop there, waiting for the light to change, and dripping and spewing debris on the road. Much the same as heavily traveled areas of city streets. Light drizzle or the first rain after periods of dry will make these areas especially hazardous.

Can we understand and anticipate all of this ahead of time, or do we have to try reacting to the sudden loss of traction and subsequent skid and crash, to gain experience.

How about the limited accesses road, on and off ramp. Are the tires working harder on these

sharp corners? Are the tires on the side of the
weight transfer being pressed down onto the pavement? Are the tires leaving tiny bits of rubber on
the road surface, especially in hot climates? During heavy traffic periods do vehicles frequently stop
or slow to a crawl in these areas? How many mil-
lion tires a year and drops of fluid are being
ground into the road surface? Sharp corners on
country roads and highways are effected much the
same way by the tires of every vehicle that passes
over them.

On a straight stretch of road your tire traction
may feel as good in the rain as it does in the dry. Is
that a false sense of security?

Do you need to understand the continually
changing road surface areas to remain in control?

Do you need to get into a deadly skid on a slippery corner to gain experience?

Do you need to jump off a three story building
to understand what is going to happen when you hit
the ground?

You do need to understand the ABS, (Anti Skid
Braking System). Up to this point we have focused
on understanding and controlling, conventional
braking systems, where the driver must control all
braking action that relates to the tires. We have discussed it in depth and I know, some of you, most of
you, are still going, "WOW"!

That, "WOW", for trying to understand and control the tires of our vehicles during emergency braking situations—is the why—ABS was invented and
installed on automobiles.

HOWEVER, like all other safety features on the
automobile we need to understand HOW, it works,
and WHY!

This is what ABS is designed to do. To sense impending tire skid, caused by the braking action, and release braking pressure to keep the tire rolling. Read this paragraph again.

That is why you may feel a pulsing sensation when you are applying the brakes hard. The system is releasing the braking pressure and all that mechanical linkage eventually ends up right back at the pedal easing up on the brakes, so you can keep pushing as hard as you need, to get stopped without skidding!

Read the two preceding paragraphs again.

Does an ABS equipped vehicle change driver control responsibility? Does it replace any of the driving skills we have discussed?

Remember when we talked about emergency braking techniques. I said when we were applying the brakes hard we must anticipate a skid and fix it immediately by releasing braking pressure until the tire was rolling then apply more pressure as the vehicle slowed. Nothing has changed! With or without ABS, communicate with your vehicle tires and weight transfer. If your vehicle is equipped with ABS, and it is functioning properly, there shouldn't be a braking skid, so there shouldn't be anything for you to fix. Continue to apply as much braking pressure as required with the tires rolling to stop or turn away! That's all there is to it!

The notion, that ABS and all the other traction control systems on your vehicle, will allow you to stop in a much shorter distance, or change direction at will, without regard to your tires, or existing road surface, is dangerously misleading!

These systems are there to assist you with car control. They will not do it for you! Any more than a washing machine will clean your cloths properly, if you don't know how to use it!

This is the year two thousand and one. Automobile safety technology has made phenomenal progress and saved I don't know how many lives. Awareness of and actions against driving under the influence have contributed significantly to reducing the numbers of lives lost to that problem. Yet, with all our best efforts, drivers lack of control of the vehicle, remains the leading cause of highway fatalities, injuries, and property damage.

That is why we are here trying to advance our driving skills and vehicle control capability by advancing our understanding of what the vehicle, **is about to do**.

Sure I would love to have all of you out on the skid pad for a day of hands on training. Yet, guess what? We would still spend time in the classroom, talking about the things we are discussing here. Without this you could spend all day slipping and sliding and still not improve your driving skills.

The skid pads used for training are controlled surfaces and areas. The skid pads you are driving on are called public streets and highways! With that thought uppermost in our minds, let's see what we can accomplish here, before we head out to the skid pad!

When your vehicle tires are pointed straight ahead, you can certainly demand all their available traction through braking, to slow and or stop the vehicle mass.

Can you also ask them to make a directional change, while all their available traction is being used by your braking demand? Think about that, and note, I said ask them. If we are using all of the tire traction available to stop the car and we turn the steering wheel, where are the tires going to get the traction to make the directional change? Making a directional change is a major traction demand on your vehicle tires. Keeping in mind, we are moving two to three thousand pounds or more of vehicle mass, from one direction to another, on four pieces of rubber each the size of your hand. Even at moderate speeds, we feel the weight transfer, as the mass wants to continue in the direction it is going.

During advanced driver training the 'turning and braking' and 'braking while turning' driving drills, create the most challenge for the students from all age levels, and professions.

This is also another big plus for ABS. If the driver inputs steering while using all available tire traction for braking; the ABS will automatically release brake pressure to compensate for the traction demand of steering. A word of caution here! If you jerk the steering wheel, and or over-steer you risk throwing your vehicle into a skid, that the ABS can not immediately correct!

If you are driving an automobile without ABS, and you need to change direction while braking hard,—what must you do with the brakes as you input steering? If you had the slightest doubt or hesitation about this question, go back and review. During the driving emergency, there will not be time!

While talking with drivers during driving clinics I am continually amazed at how many of them do not know for sure if their vehicles are ABS equipped or not. Many younger drivers don't know if their vehicle is front wheel drive or rear wheel drive or what difference it makes!

For the reactionary driver it doesn't make any difference. They are going to be reacting to what

the vehicle does, or at least trying to. For the anticipatory driver it does make a difference.

The pickup truck and the SUV, are typically rear
wheel drive; as such, they typically lose traction at
the rear tires under excessive braking or acceleration.

They are especially prone to this while going
around corners on slippery roads. If we understand
this we can take corrective action, BEFORE, we get
into the skid. It really isn't difficult to fix the turning
or accelerating skids, before they happen. If—we
have taken the time to understand WHY, they happen. It is very difficult to fix these types of skids, after they happen! Everyone wants to do skid-control
training! No one wants to do skid-prevention training.

A question I am frequently asked during training sessions goes something like this. "What if I'm
driving around a corner and hit a patch of black ice?"

My answer usually goes something like this.
"Wake up your passengers so they can watch the
wreck!"

I don't mean to be facetious, nor make light of a
seriously deadly situation, but what do you want me
to say?

If our vehicle tires have traction available, we can
be in control. If our vehicle tires have zero traction
available, we are into damage control! Don't start
making arbitrary additional traction demands! Do
know in which direction your tires are pointed so
when they regain some traction they take you where
you need to go. Do be prepared to drive into the
ditch or up against the guardrail. If you are driving a
front wheel drive car, you may be able to accelerate
smoothly and pull the vehicle out of the skid. You

may be able to accelerate a rear wheel drive vehicle and spin out the rear to point the front where you want to go.

You will be able to continue to focus on where you want to go and drive the vehicle to the best of its' capability and to the best of your ability!

There has been so much written about what to do if you get into a skid that I can't help but wonder, if the average driver has been seriously mislead to believe that it's not a big deal. "Turn into the direction of the skid." "Don't touch the brakes." "Accelerate smoothly." "Stay on the gas." "Stay off the gas." "Counter-steer as quickly as you can."

On slippery road surfaces, front wheel drive cars typically lose traction at the front tires. If you are driving around that left-hand corner and your front wheel drive car loses traction and begins to skid to the right, do you really want to steer in the direction of that skid?

If you keep your focus on where you want to go; will you be more apt to make the correct steering, braking, or accelerating actions required?

If you keep your focus on where you don't want to go; How will you know what actions are required to get you to where you do want to go?

I have had the marvelous good fortune of doing just about everything imaginable with an automobile in controlled environments on driving courses, race tracks, and skid pads. This is what I have to say about skid control. There were many driver control errors committed, prior to the skid. There were any number of ways the driver could have prevented the skid! There are very few guaranteed ways to fix it, especially on public roads, with other traffic and obstacles close by.

If you still insist on getting into a skid, and still insist I say something about how to get out of one, this is what I can tell you. You MUST continue to look where you want the car to go! Focus on that driving surface and not on the guard rail or the ditch. Then make the steering input, acceleration or braking input, the gear changes required to take the car there! Continue to drive the car! When you get to the nearest rest room facility, you may want to stop.

Please believe me when I say, the last thing I want to do is challenge my skid control skill on a public road or highway. WHY? Because I can't tell you how it is going to come out and if it comes out wrong innocent lives are at stake!

Vehicles do not cause skids! Drivers cause skids!

With that thought in mind and the understanding we have gained about vehicle control it's a good time to discuss the differences between front wheel drive and rear wheel drive vehicles.

Front wheel drive means the front tires pull the vehicle. Rear wheel drive means the rear tires push the vehicle.

"So what"

Anticipatory driving is the "So what".

If you are driving in a straight line and apply enough acceleration to spin the tires what is a rear wheel drive vehicle going to do? What is a front wheel drive vehicle going to do? Which vehicle will most likely require corrective steering to correct the spinning skid you created? What driver responses, in order of action, are required in either vehicle to correct the spinning tire skid?

First: Continue to look where you want to drive!

Second, and while you are doing the first: Give the tires back the traction you took away! I did not say jerk the foot off the pedal. I said give back the traction you took away!

Third: Make the **required** steering corrections quickly and smoothly. If the first step didn't happen, this one won't either.

What actions will you take if situation one occurs while driving around a corner?

What do you anticipate either type vehicle to do in situation one if you apply the brakes hard enough to create a braking skid on a non-ABS vehicle? Remember; on front wheel drive vehicles the front tires typically skid and not the rear tires. On rear wheel drive vehicles the rear tires or both front and rear tires typically skid.

What actions will you take for the braking skids? If your suggested sequence of actions differ from the actions of situation one you need to review.

Answer all the above questions for an ABS equipped vehicle.

What corrections would you make if the spin out or skidding were caused by excessive and harsh steering?

The anticipation and subsequent driver action will be different in all cases. The sequence of actions will be the same! **Look, see, have traction, use traction.**

> It is much easier to use the traction if we don't have to go through the process of losing it and then getting it back. That takes a long time and considerable space.

Chapter Seven

SITUATION "A"—SOLUTION "B"

In this chapter there is another driving problem I want to discuss that continues to claim lives.

Driver over-reaction to going off the traveled road surface, by accident or design.

Ditches and highway median areas are drivable (my word) terrain! Not preferable terrain for sure, but drivable! As opposed to power poles, large trees, large animals, embankments, buildings, concrete abutments, and other vehicles!

While driving down the road at highway speed, would you ever suddenly jerk the steering wheel into a full left or right turn? If any of you answered yes to this one send the book back, I can't help you.

Why then, do so many drivers do exactly that the moment their vehicle tires get into the gravel or dirt along the shoulder of the road?

Once your tires are onto the low traction environment, all it takes is a jerk of the steering wheel, to send the vehicle out of control.

When asked at driving clinics, even young inexperienced drivers answer that question correctly, yet it continues to happen at an alarming rate.

I believe the problem stems, at least in part, to the fact that we have all been told what to do if we should end up with our tires off the pavement in the dirt or gravel. Yet, we don't actually understand why.

There are various text-book solutions, but they all go something like this. Don't touch the brakes. Lift smoothly off the accelerator and steer gradually back onto the road. If the pavement has a drop off of several inches or more, steer away from that edge a foot or so and approach at a slightly sharper angel until you regain the road surface.

Does that sound about right to you? Is that your impression of what the recommended correct response should be? I certainly find no fault with that solution. It's just that, like most solutions, the solution is not the problem. The problem is, we did not drive calmly off the road to experience the correct solution. We found ourselves suddenly off the road! Where we have practiced all our driving lives never to be! We can feel the gravel crunching under our tires and rocks and grass and stuff flying! We feel a desperate loss of control and we want back on the highway! Like—Now! Our heart rate is up and those body chemicals are being dumped into the blood stream directly to our muscles! In a word, we have been seriously startled. To make matters worse, we are somewhere with our vehicle, we have never intended to be. Reactionary driving is what we instinctively revert to, and in a fraction of the time it took you to read this, we have reacted, turning back toward the road surface where we want to be, where we are looking! Only it wasn't a turn, it was a violent jerk of the steering wheel.

Remember why we always look where we want to go? Why we focus on that? The moment you left the road, you do not want to be instantly back on the road. Don't look there, don't think about it! Look at where you are driving and continue to drive the vehicle. You are driving on the shoulder of the road. The vast majority of the time it is not a horrible place to drive! In fact, many road shoulders are designed and carefully maintained for that exact eventuality! Continue to drive your car, when it is time to drive back on the road you will do so.

Here is the why. This is what your vehicle tires and weight transfer would like to tell you. Let's go back to those four pieces of rubber and the tire surface contact area. If you left the pavement on the right side of the road, the two right tires are on a low traction surface. The two left tires are on a high traction surface. The shoulder is lower than the road surface so some weight transfer takes place to the right side tires.

In this condition, can the vehicle continue to travel straight ahead without difficulty? I didn't say there was a concrete bridge abutment directly ahead. I asked a question and the answer is of course.

Can the vehicle be turned quickly and sharply to the left? Keeping in mind when this happens which tires are we asking to do the most work because they are receiving the weight transfer? The tires on the right side, the tires in the gravel! To make matters worse imagine the left front tire gripping the road

and pulling the front of the vehicle to the left and
swinging the rear to the right. Now both rear tires
are in the gravel and the vehicle is facing across the
road instead of straight ahead. Now the right front
tire makes contact with the road. One of two things
is going to happen. The vehicle launches at the speed
it is traveling, in the direction it is pointed, which is
across the road! Alternatively, the vehicle mass wants
to continue straight ahead and pulls the vehicle, now
sideways, with it. Which more than likely will result
in a roll over!

Should we slam on the brakes? If any of you are
unsure about that question, I give up!—Thank you,
I'll continue.

There is a good chance that some of you have
never driven on grass, dirt, or gravel, but a lot of us
have and continue to do so on a daily basis. We start,
stop and change direction. We understand that our
vehicle is on a low traction environment so we do it
gently. Just because you are suddenly off the road
does not mean that you can't continue to drive. It
does not mean you can't use the brakes, the accelerator or the steering wheel. It means you have to
do it, as if you were on a low traction surface. Because you are! Be gentle and keep the tires rolling
and pointed in the direction you SHOULD go.

Let's think about that last sentence for a moment.

Imagine you are driving in the dirt, grass, gravel,
or sand. Look down on the tire surface, contact area.
It is pressed slightly down into these types of surfaces.
Now turn your front tires quickly to the left. The
traction is not there to overcome the weight of the
vehicle mass so it continues straight ahead, dragging
your tires with it. In the dirt, the tire becomes a plow.

The dirt builds up in front of that plow, which with the tires turned is the side of the tire, until it makes a bank of dirt the tire can't slide sideways through. Now the rear tires are being slid sideways and they become plows. When the build up stops the tire and the vehicle mass is still going, the vehicle trips and begins to roll over.

Do not let your tires slide sideways on soft surfaces and turn into plows, because they will. That bank of dirt may stop the tire. It can not stop the vehicle mass.

A tire that is rolling or spinning is less likely to become a plow. If you end up off the road and your vehicle is losing directional stability; that is, it is beginning to slide sideways; controlled acceleration and steering will move the tires forward, and or create some tire spin, that will reduce the chance of them becoming plows. **Controlled acceleration and steering** are the key words here.

Is your vehicle automatically going to flip over or crash because it left the driving surface by accident or design? Do you understand what is happening to your vehicle tires? Do you understand where the vehicle mass is headed and how much traction the tires need to change the direction of that mass? Do you understand that no matter how badly you may want the tires to change the direction of your vehicle they may not be able to do that! You will have to straighten them out, keep them rolling, and try something else. Do you understand you must continue to drive your vehicle to the moment and point of impact if that is your only remaining option!

If you do understand that, then we have done all we can do, to insure, to the best of our ability, that moment never comes.

Right now, some of you if not most of you have some serious questions and you want to paint me into a corner. Please feel free to do so because you are coming with me.

"If I am driving down the interstate at 65 MPH and another vehicle changes lanes and forces me off the road, how can I control my vehicle off the road at that speed?"

Wow—remind me not to ride with you! You're bad luck.—Just kidding. Tough question, but here goes.

You may or may not be able to control your vehicle in that situation, but you did say you were forced off the road so off the road it is! All I can tell you, is don't turn a difficult situation into a hopeless situation; the moment you leave the road.

You see,—that is the problem with situation A, which is your situation, and solution B, which was the textbook driving solution, which is absolutely the correct solution. Remember, don't touch the brakes, lift smoothly off the accelerator and steer gradually back onto the road surface. The problem is, it doesn't quite fit, your immediate situation!

There are far too many driving situations and possible driving solutions for us to have time to go through that card index and pull one out that works.

I know you don't want to hear this again, but you are going to.—Continue to drive your vehicle, to the best of your ability.

Do you want to impact something at 65 MPH or would it be better to impact at 35 MPH? Would it be better to impact head on, or a glancing blow? Would it be better to jerk the steering wheel and put the vehicle into a skid, and a probable roll over, or steer the vehicle in a direction the tires can take you?

Would it be better to slam on the brakes and hope for the best, or continue to drive and look for the best, and maybe, just maybe, drive through this situation?

You see—If you paint me into a corner, or if I paint myself into a corner, I'm either going to wait for the paint to dry, or walk across the wet paint!— But then again, I may have some options none of us thought of, if I look around and don't slip on the wet paint!

This is a position I am going to paint myself into,— And I'm going to stay here until the paint dries!

> *Take all of your driving solutions B,—For all those driving situations A, and trade them in on a thorough understanding, of what your vehicle is capable of, and what you, the driver, are capable of! Now adjust your driving habits accordingly and please don't ever drive blindly into a situation you know you can't correct!*

I am going to give you another driving situation that continues to claim lives.

We are driving around a corner faster than we realized and the vehicle begins sliding towards the edge of the road! Think about what your tires are doing and where the weight of the vehicle mass is dragging them!

In this situation, what options do you have?

Don't say, "wake up the passengers so they can watch the wreck!" Not yet anyway.

Our tires have told us they can't handle the conditions they are in. Can we lighten their load by lessening the steering input ever so slightly? Do you have a foot or so of road to work with? Can you use that extra foot of road space to widen the steering arc instead of adding steering, which your tires have already told you they can't handle? Can we understand what is going to happen, if in spite of our best efforts, the tires contact the low traction surface along the edge of the road?

Do you want to spin out across the road or crash into the ditch, or would it be better to drive into the ditch?

Do we all understand what we are talking about here? Do not do something that isn't going to work, and in fact will make the situation far worse, because of some deeply ingrained, pre-conceived notion, that we must stay on the road at all cost!

During the driving scenario I gave you, once you used all available road space, you were going in the ditch, but you were not out of options. Your other options were how did you want to go into the ditch and how did you want to drive while you were there.

We have all been told, seen evidence of, and read in print, over, and over again, that speed kills!

Why do we refuse to accept that fact!

It doesn't just happen to the reckless driver. It happens to the careful driver, who is late for work, or some other important engagement. It happens to the inexperienced driver, who is just loving life and the automobile and goes into a corner too fast. It happens to the innocent driver, who becomes the victim of another driver.

A word of CAUTION! You ended up in the ditch because you were driving too fast! I want you in the ditch continuing to drive your vehicle. I don't want you spinning across the road and crashing into an innocent driver!

Actually, I want you to understand the difficulty of the available options and the dangers of thinking that situation 'A' can be easily solved by solution 'B'.

I also want you to understand should you become the innocent victim; with another vehicle spinning towards you; don't stare at that vehicle; look for the escape route and TURN AWAY!

If you have time to turn the steering wheel, you have options!

If you have time to 'slam on the brake', you have time to look for somewhere else to take the car and turn the steering wheel!

Are we beginning to put the ingredients together? Do we understand it takes all of the ingredients? If a single ingredient is missing, is the result going to turn out well. Do we understand the critical ingredients?

I really do hope so because you now have the recipe. The remainder of the discussion will be directed towards using and improving the recipe!

What we are going to do next is something I wasn't going to do when we first began the discussion, but I can see now it might be helpful. So here goes.

I am going to drive the scenario I gave you. Please keep in mind the only time I would enter a corner with the slightest uncertainty would be on a race track.

We are driving down a two lane road approaching a left corner. The right shoulder is three feet of gravel with a ditch after that then a brushy area, then trees. As I enter the corner, I suddenly realize I'm traveling too fast as the vehicle begins to drift to the right edge of the road. I don't even glance at the ditch and I stay on the accelerator as I let some steering out trying to unload some of the weight from the right front tires. I continue to look down the road and I am actually steering slightly towards the edge of the road. I have about two feet to use before the shoulder. The brakes are not even a consideration at this time. Nor is increasing the steering demand by trying to steer away from the ditch because my tires are just hanging on. I ease down on the accelerator in hopes of having enough traction to move forward and transfer some weight back to the center of the vehicle. It doesn't work and I slide closer to the edge of the road. I stay on the accelerator and continue looking down the road while I use the last foot of asphalt to let out more steering trying to ease the weight transfer from the right tires and get some traction. Spinning out is not an option I wish to take at this time. I am unable to stop the slide and at the moment my right side tires are about to contact the gravel I look at the shoulder and drive there and know instantly that's not going to work and straighten the steering wheel and drive into the ditch where my full focus is now directed. Dirt and rocks are flying, the right side of my car is scraping along the bank and my right mirror is ripped off. I am holding the steering wheel hard and steering into the ditch and applying some brakes gently as the vehicle slows and more brakes as it comes to a halt in the ditch. Fortunately for me the ditch was maintained and no large rock or trees were there to crash into or flip the car over.

There is another option I may have tried. As I enter the corner and realize I am traveling too fast, I steer in a straight line and brake hard using all available road space to dump ten or more miles an hour in a car length or two, then ease off the brakes and steer around the corner while continuing to brake gently. If the tires can't handle the braking demand, I'll continue to let up. I may try to accelerate smoothly. I do not look at the ditch because I am not ready to be there yet.

That whole driving situation is a problem because of the vehicle mass wanting to pull the car off the road and the suspension accepting the weight transfer as best it could. The inside tires were light and the outside tires were overloaded, so all driving efforts were directed at trying to shift the weight back to center and reduce the effects on the tires. Sometimes it works, sometimes it doesn't.

If I had looked at the ditch I would have jerked the wheel or steered away and that would have made the weight transfer worse and I would have spun out or crashed sideways into the ditch.

There is an option many drivers have in similar situations but don't understand. As I approached the corner I more than likely realized I was traveling too fast. At that instant while my tires were still pointed straight ahead I would brake hard and fast while continuing to steer straight ahead for as long as I could, then let off the brakes as I input steering to enter the corner traveling much slower. I would not wait until I was in the corner and hope for the best. The same is true with freeway off ramps. Any time we can straighten the steering and brake hard, we can dump a lot of speed in a short distance because we are using all tire traction for braking. We can't steer hard and brake hard all at the same time. That's asking for more traction than the tires have. Please don't be confused by ABS. Even with an ABS equipped vehicle the tires available traction didn't change. The

ABS simply kept the brakes from locking the tire and causing a braking skid.

How many of the ingredients did we use trying to complete that recipe? Other than entering the corner too fast, what mistakes did I make in trying to control the vehicle? What would you have done differently? If you will take a few moments each day and seriously think about that, You may gain some valuable driving judgement experience, without having to pay the big price.

We are going to move on to the next discussion but I would like you to review the prior discussions as often as you need to put the recipe together.

Chapter Eight

IMPROVE YOUR DRIVING SKILL DAILY

One of the most difficult driving skills to master is that of staying focused on the task of driving while driving. I know this to be true, because it still happens to me, and I have been working on that skill for over forty years.

While behind the wheel the vast majority of us are mentally somewhere else. This is such a prevalent and dangerous habit that we can't simply shrug it off, because it is going to happen and we don't have a solution.

At the very least, let's first admit that we don't pay full time attention to our driving and remain continually conscious of that fact. When we leave the house in the morning our minds are already at work, or still in the house, or even worse, still in bed.

Try introducing yourself to the vehicle. "Good morning car". Look at your tires, this is something we should do every time we approach the automobile anyway. Promise yourself you will think about those other things somewhere else along the route to work. Near the residence is predictably a high accident rate place.

We have previously discussed other places that are also, predictably, accident prone zones. Make your own list and review it daily.

I am in no way suggesting you should daydream at designated points along your drive to or from work. However, if I tell you to pay full time attention to your driving at all times, that advice will be the first thing you will not pay attention to. What I am suggesting, is to begin looking for some positive solutions. The mere statement, "Don't day-dream while driving", is not a solution. It is a serious problem as we have discussed in detail. Find your own ways to do something about it and continue to work at it.

I have no illusions that we are going to solve this bad driving habit on the pages of this book but if we can prevent one serious injury, it is well worth the effort. It is certainly worth your time. You need to do it daily.

Here is something else I want you to do for at least the next week every time you drive. Communicate with your vehicle tires. Feel the vibrations as they roll down the road. With some practice, you will be able to feel each individual tire. Feel them grip the pavement while you're turning corners. Feel them grip the pavement while you stop. Feel the weight transfer of the vehicle body on the tires. Notice how even moderate turning, stopping and accelerating, transfers weight through the suspension to the tires.

If your body is properly positioned in the seat and your hands properly positioned on the steering wheel, you will be able to sense and feel what the tires are doing. If your elbow is on the center console and your wrist on the steering wheel, you are not going to feel much of anything. By making a serious effort to communicate with your tires, you will also be developing some positive driving habits that could save a life.

A word of CAUTION! Do not get so distracted by a new driving experience that you forget about driving the vehicle. Do work at it daily, but judiciously.

Review the chapter on driver attitude and mindset. See how you compare and what improvements you can make during your daily commutes.

Practice seeing with your eyes instead of just looking. To do that, your brain is going to have to tell your eyes what to look for. Read the last sentence again. One more time, and please don't ever forget it.

How many stop signs or yield signs for crossing or intersecting traffic are along your routine routes? What is the condition of the road shoulders, ditches and vegetation? Could you drive on, in, or through them if you had to?

These are not just some worn out and over used questions from an out of date defensive driving manual. There is a serious WHY, here. By answering them, you are to teaching your eyes to see and gaining valuable driving experience.

Anything you can do to raise your level of awareness while driving is worth doing. Understanding why you need to make this a part of your driving habit, is a big step towards improving your driving skill and safety for every one.

Many of the driving hazards that get us into trouble are time and place predictable.

Do we have to wait for the first frost of fall to figure out which areas of our daily routes are going to become hazardous?

High water and flash flooding present serious problems for motorists. Take some time before the next flood season to be able to determine the water depth.

Many city streets that are prone to flooding have depth markers that many drivers never see or look for. At least use some common things that are everywhere along our routes to judge water depth by if the need arises. Check your vehicle owners manual for recommended fording depths. If in doubt, find another route. If there is a safe place to park, wait for another driver with more experience to cross before attempting it yourself. If the water depth is higher than your vehicle front bumper I would seriously caution selecting another route or waiting for positive assistance before crossing. Look for floating debris on the water surface to judge the current flow. A foot of water moving quickly can exert enough pressure to sweep your vehicle away with it. Six inches of fast moving water may have the same effect. If it is a bridge, that has flooded, don't cross, unless a highway safety official has determined it safe to do so.

Another daily driving exercise I have found effective is the drive SAFE drill.

Space—Available—For—Emergencies, SAFE. Now when I say, "think safe", you know what we are talking about. While you are driving around practice the drill. Ask yourself HOW would you deal with a driving emergency if it suddenly happened. Do that in traffic, while driving around a corner, while approaching intersections, when road conditions are not clean and dry. Don't get discouraged when your space is continually invaded. By virtue of the fact, you are conscious of it, you have made a tremendous improvement in driver awareness and you will discover driving techniques to adjust for it.

As you develop a keener sense of communication with your tires, and train your eyes to see, the how will become easier and more readily available.

If you think driver body position inside the vehicle is over-stressed then put the elbow on the center console or out the window and the wrist over the steering wheel, then do the how drill. How long did it take you to get into position before you could begin to exercise car control?

A word of CAUTION again! Practice the drills when it is SAFE to do so! Do not become distracted by them! The driving drills are not games and they should not be played! They are driving drills to improve your driving skill, awareness and safety! Work at them seriously and you might be amazed at the results.

I know I'm beginning to lecture and I promised not to do that, but many drivers think driver training is something we did before we got a license, and gaining experience is something that happens automatically with time.

It is not and it does not!

Chapter Nine

THE 4X4, SUV ON THE HIGHWAY

The four-wheel drive pick up truck or sport utility vehicle, (SUV) is a great automobile to drive. I have driven them for years and love their versatility. However, there are many drivers, who don't happen to share my appreciation for this vehicle. In fact, when they are improperly driven, by inconsiderate drivers, I don't much care for them either!

Before we get into the vehicle handling characteristics and driver control, let's take some time to talk about driving etiquette. All you 4x4, SUV drivers don't go fast forward to the good stuff. Stay with me for awhile, because there are drivers out there who hate your vehicle. All you, non-SUV types, hang around too, because there is good information for you.

For the sake of this conversation, I am going to refer to SUV as any vehicle that is substantially taller and larger than the average car.

Because your SUV allows you to see farther down the road than the driver of the car in front of you, does that mean, you can follow closer or stop quicker? Think about what the driver in front of you is seeing in the rear view mirrors of their car. Nothing but bumper, grill and headlights! Is that what you like to see in your rear view mirrors? I think not. I certainly don't. The SUV driver must understand, you are sharing the road, not only physically, but also emotionally and psychologically as well. You may be up above the crowd looking around and loving life, but the driver in front of you is becoming upset to the point of becoming a hazard!

Please don't tell me that, "That's the other drivers problem", because it is not. No more than, "driving under the influence" is the drunk drivers problem! These things are all our problems by virtue we all must share the road together.

Maintain enough space between your SUV and the car in front, so the driver of that vehicle can see other lanes of traffic to the rear, and your smiling face.

I have ridden with SUV drivers who get all upset because the car in front of them is being driven jerkily and the brake lights are continually on and off. The other driver might be trying to tell you something.

"That's all well and good, but if I back off, some other car is just going to cut in!"

More than likely, you are correct. For me, that is all a part of driving the vehicle of my choice. Much the same as any motor bike driver accepts the problems of driving their vehicle of choice and makes the necessary adjustments.

The cars behind your SUV are also at a considerable disadvantage. Those drivers will have to back off three to four times the normal following distance to see ahead, and we all know that is not going to happen during rush hour traffic. Because the SUV driver can see farther ahead, this should allow you to alert the drivers following to potential hazards. Make every effort you can to alert the driver back there, to driving conditions ahead, and make that a part of your SUV driving habits.

If you drive an SUV, accept the responsibility that goes with your choice of vehicle and enjoy the experience. Don't let bad driving habits make your SUV, a DUV, (dumb utility vehicle).

Car drivers pay attention! When you find an SUV driver who is trying to be considerate, don't put yourself right in front of them and then get upset because they are too close. I don't have all the solutions. We all know all the problems, and by virtue of that, we all know, we have to be the solutions.

The 4x4, SUV is not the car you learned to drive in!

We know it is at the tires where everything happens, so let's start there. They are taller than your average car tires, with generally taller tire side walls. This means the correct inflation pressure is especially critical to keep the tread contact surface area pressed onto the pavement during cornering and stopping. Think about the effect weight transfer had on our tires during some of the earlier scenarios and add a couple of inches of side wall to that. Because the vehicle body is taller, the weight transfer will be greater.

Here again folks, we are not going to get into scientific formulas and definitions. Right now, I want you to mentally visualize how your tires are being effected by this taller vehicle mass.

Those of you that can calculate all that are one step ahead of the discussion and that's fine. For those who can't, like myself, and I suspect, most of you, we are going to walk through how it works until we understand it and are able to calculate it, in a slightly different manner.

The very first time you sat in an SUV you had a different sense of height than you did in your car. When you drove it around the very first corner, you had a different sense of balance. Your body was telling you something.

Those of you who got all excited because what you felt was a sense of power and strength, are the scary ones, and the ones the car drivers love to hate.

We discussed in detail the effect on our vehicle tires surface contact area when the driver jerked the steering wheel or over steered and threw the weight onto the suspension system and the tires. Now multiply that from modest to severe, depending on the height and weight of the particular 4x4 or SUV. We discussed how a sliding tire in the dirt could plow up enough of a bank to trip the car and cause a roll over. Think about how much easier it is to trip a taller vehicle. This also applies to vans and mini vans!

We talked about the difference between front wheel drive and rear wheel drive while driving around corners. The 4x4, SUV, is a rear wheel drive vehicle when not in four wheel drive, which on hard surface roads is all the time. The pick up truck 4x4 is a rear wheel drive vehicle with more weight to the front than to the rear, causing the rear tires to lift more easily and lose traction more easily.

The effects of speed and wind and the amount of lift caused by rushing air over the vehicle are also greater on these types of vehicles than on cars.

During multiple directional weight changes, the taller, longer, more weight forward vehicle is effected to a much greater degree than the smaller car. We have all seen car drivers whipping in and out of traffic, changing lanes rapidly, and we all know that is reckless at best. In the 4x4, SUV, it is a serious loss of control waiting to happen.

Imagine what is happening to the tires as the weight is thrown from side to side. Imagine that on a slippery road surface. Ever wonder why 4x4, SUV drivers end up in the ditch on a snow covered road. It has nothing to do with vehicle capability. It has everything to do with driver misunderstanding and subsequent lack of skill because they don't understand their vehicle limitations!

Speaking of limitations, many of you may be tempted to go to larger and or more aggressive tread type tires, because it looks rugged and because they are better in the mud. Well they do and they are, but think about how much you have decreased the tire surface contact area on hard surface roads! Serious off road drivers understand the trade off and adjust driving habits on paved roads.

All of the car control skills we discussed apply to the SUV even more so. The SUV is a great vehicle, for those that need or want the versatility. It is not a sedan and just because you can get an SUV moving on slippery roads doesn't mean it will change direction or stop. Driving this vehicle requires all the skill, plus a greater understanding.

Chapter Ten

ELIMINATING DRIVER DISTRACTIONS

How much of a problem, do you think, driver distractions are to highway safety?

I do not believe, any of us, are of the opinion that all those fender bender accidents are caused deliberately. I also know that the percentage of highway fatalities caused by driver actions such as DUI, reckless, excessive speed, do not add up to one hundred percent of all fatalities. So there are some other serious causes out there. A large percentage one is failure to pay full time attention.

What do you consider a driver distraction to be? How long does it have to last to be hazardous to our health?

Wow, we did it again and my ears are burning, but I know none of you would do any of those crazy things while you were driving! Would you?

We are all going to be distracted, to some extent, while we are driving and that is something I don't have a complete solution for. However, when we first started driving we received some excellent advice about that. It simply ended up misinterpreted.

For many years, beginning drivers have been taught the two to three second rule for following distance and additional seconds for road conditions. That is not just stopping distance! That is total elapsed time distance! Judging from past student responses, we don't have a great deal of difficulty judging stopping distance so we begin to equate that to following distance. We do have difficulty with the total elapsed time distance. When we misjudge that, we are into our stopping distance and into a driving emergency! I would like all of us to do all of us a favor. Think and practice total elapsed time instead of stopping distance and adjust accordingly. Think and practice total elapsed time.

The passenger who spills coffee all over the interior of your beautiful car is a serious distraction! It shouldn't be. It's a done deal, there isn't anything you can do about it right then!

How many of you can change your car radio stations, volume, speaker controls, tapes or CDs without looking down at the radio? How about the air conditioning or heater controls? How about setting or picking up the soda or cup of coffee in the console tray? We could go on and on here, but the point I want to make is how far is your vehicle traveling while you are mentally inside the car, looking down, doing any of these things.

I want you to do a simple self test for me, as soon as you can, while driving or riding in a vehicle. Count aloud, one thousand and one, and see how many vehicle lengths you traveled while doing that at 25 MPH. Then do it at 35 MPH, and at 55 MPH.

Don't do it at 55 MPH in a 35 MPH speed zone! The officer writing the ticket isn't going to understand, although it may be the first time, he or she has heard that excuse.

It may take several attempts to get an accurate idea of how far your vehicle will travel in one second, but continue to conduct the test until you are certain.

Don't look it up in your drivers manual or calculate it. The figures didn't mean anything to you the first time you read them and they won't now, until you see for yourself how much road space you're using up, during that one second of time.

While your vehicle is parked, count how long it takes to do any of the things you do inside the car that take your focus off the road ahead. You competitive types, don't make this a game or contest and don't fudge on the outcome. This is for you, and me if I'm the person you run off the road while changing your CD!

If this exercise doesn't cause you to seriously evaluate the self induced driver distractions, then you didn't do the exercise or you are deluding yourself. I have been timing driver distractions for years, and it's scary!

Changing the settings on your car air conditioner, from MAX to a setting where the air will flow on the floor and out the vents, takes from one and a half to two seconds. I have timed drivers who spend a full three seconds fiddling with the knob or lever.

I am not going to tell you how far the vehicle traveled during those three seconds because I want you to experience for yourself, so you will believe it, and begin to do something about it.

I DID NOT SAY TO GO DRIVE FOR THREE SECOUNDS, AT ANY SPEED, WHILE LOOKING DOWN AT YOUR AIR CONDITIONER CONTROLS!

Yet I will venture to say, all of us, at some time while driving, have done something similar and because nothing bad happened that time we lull ourselves into complacency about our own driving habits. Do we have to wait until we run out luck to gain the driving experience of how disastrous a one second lapse can be?

Now that we all understand the seriousness of the seemingly innocent distractions inside the car, let's talk about how we intend to fix them.

For the younger drivers this is going to be easy because you love to sit in your car and play the radio, and touch and feel. For us veterans, we will just have to suck it up and get it done. Don't whine and snivel, and don't tell me you don't need to do this. Tell yourself, and be honest, then sneak out to the car when no one is looking so you don't have to admit you may have a bad driving habit.

This is very simple. I want you to sit in the car, in the dark and arbitrarily twist all the knobs and push all the levers and buttons until you have all vehicle accessory controls out of adjustment. DON'T run your vehicle engine inside the garage!

After that I want you to look straight ahead, where you can't see the controls and I want you to readjust them all. You don't have to memorize all the positions of the heater air conditioner controls. All you have to do is move them and feel where the air is coming from and if it is hot or cold. For some of us this may take some time, so take all the time you need. While sitting in a parked car, manipulating accessory controls, we have all the time in the world.

Once the car is in motion, we don't have time for distractions.

I'm going to tell a short story to illustrate how I feel about this.

"Yesterday evening my sixteen year old son was heading out the door to go to his part time job. I noticed he had some gadgets in his hand and inquired what they might be. He proudly displayed a CD player adapter he had saved for and purchased. It plugs into the car tape player so he can play his CDs. I went outside with him, watched as he plugged it in, set it up, and inserted a CD. I listened approvingly to some horrible sounds my fifty-six year old ears didn't recognize as music, but that's cool. What wasn't so cool was the fact he couldn't insert the CD without looking at the player resting on the passenger seat. It required over a second to slip it in and snap the lid. We talked about that and he agreed to not change the disc while driving until he could do it by feel."

I'm going to ask you to do a few things for me and you are going to think I have taken a full left turn, at 60 MPH!

Imagine you are sitting in your living room chair with a hot cup of coffee and you are about to have a sip. Just before it gets to your lips, DROP IT!

"NO WAY!"

If you are driving down the road about to take a sip, and the driving emergency occurs, how long is it going to take you to set the cup down? Drop it, on the passenger floor!

I do not want to receive some legal notice from your lawyer because you threw scalding coffee on your passenger because I told you to. I didn't tell you to. I asked you to think about it now, while we have time.

I love my morning coffee, and afternoon and evening to, but mine is going on the passenger floor without a second thought, if necessary! I say passenger side because we don't want anything rolling around under our feet at a time like this! Think about it.

This one is going to get me in trouble for sure, but I want you to do the same exercise with your cellular telephone.

"DOUBLE NO WAY!"

Think about it! If it is in our car, the cellular telephone controls become vehicle accessory controls, and we need to spend some time with them, in the dark, or upgrade our equipment to hands free, eye free, operation. Period, and end of that conversation.

Some of you are saying bad things about me and you shouldn't be. You can fix it and you should!

I have a cellular telephone and I have the choice of when to make or receive calls. I also have the understanding of the serious consequences of misusing this marvelous piece of modern day equipment while driving.

The only thing I am advocating here is "Drive SAFE". Remember what the letters stand for, "Space—Available—For—Emergencies,   and understand, when the vehicle is in motion, time is space. How long did you say it took you to dial that call, and how long were your eyes off the road to do that?

There are many other driving distractions I am certain you can think of and correct if you will take the time to do it.

My big distractions are those 'FRESH DONUT' signs. I can smell 'em and taste 'em right now, but I have fixed the distraction problem. When I see one I close my eyes until I'm past.

Just kidding folks, but then again, isn't that close to what we do when we are searching intently for an address or a particular store.

Don't start on me again, I am not chastising you for doing something while driving that is going to occur on a routine basis. What I would like us to do is get away from the notion that we have to find it and turn into it, all at the same time. Alternatively, that if we miss it because we were focused on driving, we won't ever find it again.

Something you might find helpful is knowing the numbering system that all major cities and munici-palities have. If you are looking for 1254 West Broad street, it will be between 12th and 13th street on the West Side of town. After the numerical streets, the numbering system continues letters or names, in al-phabetical order. This system starts somewhere near the city center and goes outward, North, South, East and West. Major boulevards or natural barriers such as rivers will be the dividing lines. On all streets and Boulevards, odd numbers will be on one side and even numbers will be on the other. If you see 957 on a building on the right, you are between 9th and 10th street, so you have two blocks to go and 1254 is going to be on the left. Some large cities are further defined by sections. For example in our nation's capitol, the city is divided into four sections. NW, NE, SW, SE and each section are identically numbered, within the section.

The point of all this is don't get in a wreck at 3rd street trying to find 1254 by trying to look at both sides of the street and drive at the same time. By the same thought process, don't drive distracted searching for an address that is 15 blocks down the boulevard. Don't go looking for a name when you could have gotten an address. If you are asking for directions also ask for an address. The red car in the driveway next door might have moved.

It honestly is not that difficult, for us to do everything we can to eliminate driver distractions, PRIOR to the distraction, and I sincerely hope we understand the WHY of that one.

Another important driving skill to help us avoid visual distractions is to improve our peripheral vision.

"Yep, here it comes again. How many times have we all heard this one?"

Not at all, in fact I want to take some of the myth out of this peripheral vision thing. We can not look in two directions at once. We can see in more than one direction at a time.

You are standing at the kitchen counter buttering a slice of bread and someone enters the room within your field of vision. Can you see the person while looking at the slice of bread and continuing to spread the butter?

If we are serious about improving our driving skills, and we know there are going to be times when we must look one way and see another, doesn't it behoove us to practice doing that, and gaining experience, 'PRIOR TO'?

As in all else we have discussed, there will not be time during the highway emergency to practice. We will have to get it right the first time. I strongly encourage you to gain all the experience and understanding you can, the easy way.

The actual in-car emergency, normally related to children or other passengers, is a serious driver distraction. Here are some things I would like you to think about to prepare for this one, because it is going to take all of our attention back inside the car and it is probably going to keep it there.

First–Think—SAFE. The letter, "S", means space. Create that as quickly as possible. Don't slam on the brakes and create additional driving emergencies. The moment we lift off the accelerator pedal we are creating space to the front as we slow. The moment we turn on the emergency flashers we alert other drivers to give us space to the rear and sides. That does not mean they instantly can, or will.

Off accelerator—On Flashers! The next time you get in your vehicle, while it is parked, it might be a good idea to manipulate the flasher control a few times, without looking at it.

A choking sound from a back seat passenger is a serious startle to any driver! The reason I say, "off accelerator—on flashers" is to put our minds and bodies into a series of positive actions to control those body chemicals that can shut us down, or cause us to do things to make matters worse!

The first action required less than a second of time, because we had prepared for it. We still have plenty of time and we are scared but in control!

How is our "Space"? Is it "Available" "For" the "Emergency"?

What we do next is going to depend on the driving environment.

Continue to drive the vehicle. Count off the seconds aloud if it helps. Bringing our vehicle to a controlled stop once the way is clear, onto the shoulder of the road, will take less than ten seconds, even at highway speeds. We must continue to take positive controlled actions and it will be easier now because those chemicals are working for us instead of against us.

Whatever our situation and subsequent decision let's not throw away all of our options in the first half second. Good decisions while driving require good information. It is all there for us and we can assimilate it and respond to it in fractions of seconds. "IF"— We have prepared ourselves prior to!

There is another serious driver distraction that has surfaced in recent months as I have been working on this book. Apparently, some of us don't understand warning and regulatory signs and complicated traffic signals. If we are talking about you, don't deny it, do something about it. There is a Department of Motor Vehicles where you can get the information. You can get it from your local high school. You can get it with your computer on line. You can get it from the American Automobile Association. Those moments of confusion about signs and signals are causing an increased number of traffic crashes.

Denial is a serious mental block to developing anticipatory driving skills and an even greater obstacle to putting those skills to work!

Chapter Eleven

LET'S GO DRIVE

We are driving in the country on a clear day with a front wheel drive non-ABS equipped car. The road is two lanes and posted for 55 MPH with narrow shoulders and shallow ditches on either side, then fields of mature corn. We enter a right hand corner and midway through the turn is a farm tractor with a broken wheel and a large truck is approaching in the on coming lane!

Write down, in sequence, your driving actions and your anticipation of vehicle response, to avoid a crash. (My solutions will be at the end of the chapter.)

Drive the same scenario in an SUV and write down the solutions and anticipated vehicle reactions.

Answer each scenario again for a wet rainy day.

After surviving the first scenario, we are continuing along at highway speed. The right front tire contacts a broken piece of pavement and suddenly jerks the vehicle onto the shoulder of the road and partially into the cornfield.

Write down in sequence your driving actions and anticipated vehicle response. You don't have to build anything into the scenario.

Do the same scenario with an SUV.

I am going to give you a situation that actually happened to me. I was driving on a three lane boulevard at 45 MPH in the middle lane looking for an address on the right. I chose the middle lane to avoid vehicles stopping unexpectedly to make right turns while I was distracted looking for the address. At the same moment I saw the address I caught a flash of brake lights from the vehicle to my front out of the corner of my eye. I was immediately on the brakes as hard as I could, short of skid, and knew instantly I couldn't stop in time. What would your response have been and why?

My solutions for Let's Go Drive

Going around the right turn, my tires had traction available so I am on the brakes quickly, but not as hard as I would be while traveling in a straight line. Anticipating a front wheel skid, I am ready to release pressure if required but I continue to press the brake pedal harder as the vehicle slows. I am looking for an escape route to the right into the cornfield if I can't get stopped. I am not looking at the tractor because that is not where I want to be stopped. I am looking a few feet my side of the tractor and towards the right edge of the road. I am gradually steering in that direction. If I can't stop by that point, I will release the brakes, look into the cornfield and drive around the tractor on the right side. Most likely,

I will be accelerating smoothly as I do this to keep the vehicle moving forward, not sideways. If the vehicle were ABS equipped, I would have done the exact same thing. If you are not certain about impending skid and have ABS, then you should simply push hard on the brake pedal and let the ABS do it's job of preventing the skid. However, stay in communication with the tires just in case the ABS decided to take the day off.

With the SUV, the only change would be to anticipate a rear wheel skid or perhaps both front and rear wheel and fix it quickly by releasing braking pressure then making smooth corrective steering input if need be. Most rear wheel skids can be fixed by letting up on the brakes and no steering is required if we do it quickly before the skid sends the vehicle sideways. Be prepared to get off the brakes and drive into the cornfield if you get into a skid you can't control. What you don't want is to overcorrect and have the vehicle spin the other way and end up out in front of the oncoming truck. ABS is a big help with the rear wheel drive vehicles because it allows the driver to be more aggressive with the brakes and allows the rear brakes to work harder because the ABS will correct any skidding tire.

On a wet rainy day, everything is going to be done more gently and with more concern for skid because you won't have time or traction to fix it if you slid out in front of the oncoming truck. My focus on a wet road would probably be towards the cornfield sooner. In this scenario that's the safest place to be. ABS is especially valuable on a wet road surface while turning, because it monitors each tire.

If your solutions differ from mine, as far as what the vehicle is going to do or can do, you need to go back and review. If they differ as far as selected options, I can't argue with that, unless you opted to impact the truck or the tractor. There were better options.

For the next scenario my only concern would be to keep the vehicle moving forward and not get sideways. I would stay on the accelerator or lift only modestly if the need arose and drive back on the road as soon as I safely could.

For my driving situation I lifted off the brakes and drove around to the right hoping the way was clear. I did not have time to look in the side mirror and I did not want to impact the car stopped in front of me at the speed I was traveling. Fortunately, the driver in the right lane was paying attention and made room for my escape route. I thanked that driver profusely! That was my driving decision. The situation was created by my thinking no one was going to suddenly stop in the middle lane. I was wrong.

You can write scenarios for yourself and your friends and you can do the, 'what would I do', driving drills.

Think about driving your vehicle through the situations we have discussed. Think about what would happen if you or your passengers were not wearing seat belts? Even if you refuse to accept the fact that seat belts save lives. You must accept the fact; you can not drive while being tossed about. You can't drive if your passengers are tossed about and end up in your lap.

Think S A F E! Look for the escape route that offers the path of least resistance! Always look, look and see! Continue to drive your vehicle!

It would not hurt any of us to review those defensive driving manuals that have been collecting dust. If you can't find them contact your DMV or AAA club. There is a lot of good information. You can now relate to it.

There are good courses offered all over the country to enhance driver education and training.

Advanced driver training should be conducted **ONLY under the supervision of a qualified instructor on a controlled driving course.**

> **Contact   THE   COMLETE DRIVER.COM web site for information on advanced driving courses, community development of driving courses and any questions or comments you wish to post on the message boards.**

Chapter Twelve

UNANSWERED DRIVING QUESTIONS

"Why are under inflated tires so dangerous?"

Because they build up heat that can damage or destroy the rubber compounds of the tires. Lack of air volume, smooth side wall rubber in contact with the road, more rubber in contact with the road, and the distortion of the tire tread all contribute to the heat build up, as does speed. We could go into a scientific explanation of all of these factors, which would take several pages, and probably not help. Accept this fact, or research it in depth on your time and then accept it. Under inflated tires, build up more heat and the faster we go the worse it gets!

We have discussed the effects of under-inflated tires on driver car control. We're going to do it again because even as we are talking, there is an accident happening, that an improperly inflated tire is contributing to!

Low tire pressure allows the tire side wall to flex, which allows the tire tread to flex and distort, particularly during turning when side forces caused by weight transfer are trying to push the tire sideways. The advanced car control and life saving technologies of the modern day automobile can be effectively negated by one improperly inflated tire!

If you can't find the vehicle owners manual, check drivers door or door pillar, or under the hood or trunk lid for the sticker that will tell you the recommended tire size and inflation pressure. If all else fails, check the tire side wall for, 'recommended tire pressure'. Keep in mind this pressure may effect the handling characteristics of some vehicles. Treat inflation pressure as vital information and do whatever it takes to get the information and comply with the information.

Some vehicle manufacturers offer a range of tire pressure. It might be from twenty six to thirty PSI (pounds per square inch). Do you want a firm rigid side wall or a softer side wall?

I like to communicate with my tires, so vibrations transmitted from a firmer tire are a source of information to me. I also like to know that the tire surface contact area will be there for me, to the best of the design capability, when I need it. I go high side on tire inflation pressure.

"How about that tire blow out which you promised to discuss and haven't yet!"

I was hoping you had forgotten. Not at all, and I'm glad you reminded me because it would have done scant good to try and explain it before we got through all the other things that effect car control during the driving emergency. Sudden weight transfer onto a tire that has instantly gone flat is an invitation to serious loss of control. To best understand what is going to happen, let's get behind the wheel and imagine having a blow out. We are driving down the highway when our left front tire suddenly begins to shudder and pulls the vehicle violently to the left. Our first instinct is to fight the wheel and perhaps jerk it back to straight-ahead. When the left front tire lost air pressure it dropped the vehicle several inches and became a large drag. Some weight instantly transferred to the left front, which created more drag and pulled the steering wheel in that direction. When we instinctively corrected by turning right, we transferred more weight onto a tire that couldn't handle it.

The moment we realize a tire has a serious problem we need to do all we can to keep the vehicle weight off the tire and to not ask the tire to do any work. Use all the highway space you safely can to relieve that tire of its' share of the vehicle load. That may require maintaining acceleration, and easing off, as you are able to direct the vehicle in a direction to safely come to a stop. A rear tire blow out is going to cause the back of the vehicle to slew in the direction of the deflated tire. Our instincts to counter steer in this situation are probably correct, as that will transfer some of the weight to the good tire. A tread puncture type of blow out is normally more frightening than deadly, if the driver doesn't over react. Stabilize the vehicle and don't put added weight on the blown tire by steering input, braking or accelerating. Relieve the tire by smooth gentle steering input, acceleration or braking as required. Having a blow out at highway speeds is a difficult driving situation at best and I'm not going to mislead you by making you believe it is something easily controlled. It is not. If we can control our initial instincts to fight the wheel pull, while holding the vehicle under control, with all the shimmying and shaking, we have a good chance to get the vehicle slowed and safely stopped. The first second of a tire blow out is the most critical. Hang on and don't do anything arbitrarily or jerkily and that means accelerator and brakes as well as steering. Think about all the driving techniques we have discussed. Think about having your wrist loosely draped over the top of the steering wheel when the blow out spins the wheel left. A side wall blow out or a tread separation blow out will be more violent because the air in the tire is released more quickly. Do what you must to get through the blow out stage and into the driving on a flat tire stage.

"Can I drive on a flat tire if I don't think it is safe to change it where I'm at."

Continue to drive the vehicle, until it is safe to do something else!

Yes, a vehicle can be driven on a flat tire. A vehicle can be driven on several flat tires. You did say it was because of safety not because you didn't want to change it!

The wheel was in use on vehicles a long time before rubber tires were placed over the wheel. However, those vehicles traveled at slow speeds compared to modern vehicles and were hard to control and even more difficult to make change directions. Do we understand what we are talking about here?

A flat tire is going to thump and bang and shimmy and shake and send frightening vibrations through the steering wheel, but you can certainly drive on it and should, if it is unsafe to do otherwise. This means personal safety as well as vehicular safety. If creeping along on a flat tire creates safety hazards, you are going to have to ignore some of the shaking and rattling and pay close attention to the rolling. You are going to ruin the tire and perhaps the rim but that is of no consequence, where the lives of your vehicle occupants or the lives of others are at risk.

How far you can drive on a flat tire is going to depend on a number of things. First thing is how far do you need to drive to be in a safe place. Because we are discussing a controversial subject, please keep in mind, an inconvenient place is not necessarily an unsafe place.

After a few revolutions of the wheel the tire will come loose from the rim and just kind of flop along. This means if the flat is on a driving wheel, the rim will be spinning inside the loose tire and the tire will be rolling by the force of the moving vehicle. If you stop on the slightest of an incline, you may not get moving again because the rim is spinning inside the stopped tire. A flat tire on the front of the vehicle may also come completely off the rim and possibly jam up the steering linkage. Although this is unlikely, we are talking about making informed decisions.

If you have a flat tire and stopping is an obviously unsafe decision, then continue to drive the vehicle as far as you must. Proceed at a speed consistent with your ability to drive under control until it is safe to do something else. Don't expect that flat tire to do much of anything, except keep the vehicle chassis up off the ground.

Because of something as uncomplicated as having a flat tire, lives have been lost and serious injuries have occurred when drivers stopped driving and stopped thinking SAFE. What was it we said, those four letters represented, to the complete driver? Space Available For Emergencies.

Please take the time to drive safe and think safe, before, reacting arbitrarily to any driving problem, during any driving problem, and after any driving problem!

"What should I do when driving on snow or ice?"

Drive where the traction is best and at a speed dictated by available traction. Test your braking traction and steering traction at moderate speeds and adjust accordingly. Continue to test traction as you drive. During freezing rain conditions, the edges or shoulder of the road offers the best traction. Loose snow offers better traction than packed snow. Driving early in the morning while the snow is frozen offers better traction than when the surface first begins to thaw. Some tire spin may be inevitable but when the tires lose grip, lift off the accelerator until you feel them grip again. There is no magic to driving on snow. It is all about traction. Sometimes while trying to stop, the engine drive train may be driving the vehicle forward and you may have to shift into neutral to let the tires work more effectively. The same may be true when trying to turn a corner, although with front wheel drive gentle acceleration will frequently pull the car around the corner. Think traction and don't plan to use something that isn't there. Think space, lots of it. Sometimes a gentle braking action with the left foot while under acceleration will help control tire spin. Sometimes all these techniques will get you going faster than you should be and you will end up in the ditch.

"What kind of safety equipment should I keep in my car?"

During the off road portion of advanced drivers training the first question I ask students, is if they ever planned to be stuck. The response is usually guarded and quizzical, but negative. Nobody goes out driving intending to be stuck!

Well, if you have never intended to be stuck, how do you plan to be unstuck?

If you have never intended to need travel safety equipment; how do you intend to get it when you need it? We can certainly go from mild to wild when it comes to equipping our vehicles. Sit down and ask yourself: What would you need if your car broke down where you are intending to drive. What would you like to have? What if you must abandon the car?

As a minimum, you should have a complete driver and The Complete Driver should be securely fastened between the steering wheel and the seat!

DRIVE SAFE!